Peace Be Upon Ibrahim
Vol. II

A collection of memories from the life of Shaheed Ibrahim Hadi

Translated by
Sayyid Haydar Jamaludeen

Translated from the Persian book *"Salam bar Ibrahim"*
Translated by Sayyid Haydar Jamaludeen
Edited by a group of sincere lovers of the martyrs.
Book cover design by Ahmed Cherri

First edition published in 2020
ISBN: 978-1-7384949-5-8

بِسْمِ ٱللَّهِ ٱلرَّحْمَنِ ٱلرَّحِيمِ

In the Name of God,
the Beneficient, the Merciful

بسم رب الشهداء والصديقين

In the Name of the Lord
of the Martyrs and the Righteous

CONTENTS

The view of the Leader regarding Shaheed Ibrahim	1
The Tehrani Youth	2
The Role Model	8
In the Name of our Mother	10
A Servant of Allah	13
Volleyball	15
The Fight	17
The State of the Great	20
A Guide towards Sayyid ash-Shuhada (a)	23
Modesty	25
The Slap	27
Kebab and Rice	30
Guidance	31
Akhlaq	34
Friendship	35
Ignorance and Guidance	38
The Wrestling Gym	41
The Rights of the People	43
A Man of God	45
The Path of Allah	48
Encountering Evil	49
The Toyota	53
In the Presence of the Scholars	54
The Practical Tradition	57
The Religious Organisation	62
Respecting the Sayyids	64
The Red Bandanas	67
The Adhan	69
Those Four People	71
Wilayah	74
The Benefit of the Religion	77
The Guard	79
Allure	81
Jahanshah	86
Shiyakouh	88
Conqueror of the Peak	92

The Exemplary Personality	95
Allahu Akbar	98
Behind Enemy Lines	101
Insight	104
The Ya Mahdi (aj) Headband	107
The Miracle	109
Spirituality	112
Fajr in Congregation	115
O' Fatimah Zahra (a)!	116
The Good Old Days	118
Amriyyeh	121
Inside the Trench	124
The Sorrowful Days	128
Water	132
The Final Day	136
The Sincere Servant of Allah	141
The Manner of Introduction	144
Ibrahim, the Guide	146
The Brother's Invitation	148
The Guest	152
Reza	156
To Allah	158
The Child's Cure	161
The Crown of Servitude	164
Short memories from the life of a great person	168
The Protectors of the Shrine	176

THE VIEW OF THE LEADER REGARDING SHAHEED IBRAHIM

The great leader of the Revolution has always encouraged the authors of various book genres, especially books regarding the era of Holy Defence. In the many meetings he held with the authors of these books, he often emphasised several points. Commander Golali Babaei (assistant director of the Foundation of Art Preservation) refers to a meeting of a group of commanders with the Leader of the Revolution and says:

On Monday, the 5th of October 2015, we had were scheduled to meet the Leader. Commander Hamadani[1] was meant to fly to Syria on Sunday, the 4th of October, but when he heard about the meeting with the Leader, he delayed his journey. I had not heard him say this, but my friends say that he said, "Let me go and see the Leader for the last time." On Monday, he came in his military uniform. Me, Commander Kazemayni, Commander Hamadani and Commander Muhaqqeq were sitting in the front row. The Leader welcomed him and the others with a smile. When the meeting

---

[1] General Hosein Hamadani was a commander of the IRGC. He took part in the Iran-Iraq War and was pivotal in quelling the rebellions in Kurdistan. He was martyred on the 7th of October 2015 in an ISIS attack in Aleppo, Syria.

ended, the Leader started to look at the books regarding the era of Holy Defence which were organised on a shelf in the house. The Leader then started to speak about the translation of these books and he also talked about the personalities of these martyrs. He emphasised, "The martyrs whose lives were chosen for a book to be written about were martyrs whose stories are beneficial for us." He gave an example, saying, "Recently, I read a book regarding Shaheed Ibrahim Hadi *(Peace be upon Ibrahim)*, and despite finishing the book, I couldn't bring myself to put it down." By giving such an example, he emphasised on personalities who could have biographies and novels written about them.

THE TEHRANI YOUTH

Words of Shaykh Panahian when remembering the martyrs of the Kumayl Trench on the Day of Youth, May 2015

Shaheed Ibrahim Hadi is a prominent martyr amongst the two hundred and fifty thousand that we gave as a sacrifice during the era of Holy Defence. I advise the people and youth who haven't already read this book to definitely study it. I assure them that their views and *akhlaq* will be different after they read this book, and they can even divide their life into two parts: one before reading this book and one after reading this book! I am not exaggerating. I am sure that whoever reads this book and gets to know this personality will agree with me. Ayatollah al-Udhma Bahjat (ra) said, "Studying the lives of the great people holds the same position as taking a class in *akhlaq*." By studying this book, you will feel a spiritual effect on your being. The position of our martyrs is protected by Allah and we are unaware of this position.

Perhaps there are many martyrs from the era of Holy Defence whose statuses are higher than Shaheed Ibrahim Hadi and we do not know them, but Allah wanted us to know personalities such as Ibrahim Hadi. Allah wanted him to live in one of the neighbourhoods in the centre of Tehran, to be one of the youths of our city who is different from the others, and this difference is clear. Shaheed Hadi was neither a religious scholar nor was he considered a commander of the era of Holy Defence (according to the literal meaning of the word), but rather he was one of the masses. His blessed father was an ordinary businessman and worked as a shopkeeper. Perhaps one of the characteristics that distinguished him from others was that he was a complete athlete. The *akhlaq* that Shaheed Ibrahim Hadi displayed in the ring of the gym is presented in this book and was also displayed later on the warfront.

The epics of the Kumayl Trench are prominent amongst the great moments of the era of Holy Defence, but the Kumayl Trench takes pride in Shaheed Ibrahim Hadi. This martyr is an eternal source of pride for the Kumayl Trench. If the people of Tehran want to use one of their good people as an example, it is better if they use Shaheed Ibrahim Hadi as an example and say, "A Tehrani youth like Shaheed Hadi." Perhaps many of the good people of Tehran will enter heaven following in the footsteps of Shaheed Ibrahim Hadi. You know that Shaykh Dulabi (ra) wouldn't exaggerate; when he saw Ibrahim Hadi, a twenty-year-old youth, he waited for the crowd to disperse. He then said to Ibrahim Hadi, "Ibrahim! Give me some advice!" and Ibrahim lowered his head out of embarrassment as if to say, "Shaykh! What are you saying?!" However, in my opinion, Shaykh Dulabi (ra) said these words with belief.

In your opinion, other than Ibrahim Hadi, who is the prominent youth of Tehran from the time of the Revolution? If anyone wants to see an example of the revolutionary generation, they must look no further than Ibrahim Hadi. This is based on the information that we have received. When you look at the sky, some of the stars are brighter as they are closer to us. Of course, there are also greater stars, but further away from us and we can't see their light clearly. Therefore, those stars which are closer to us are our guides like the North Star and we find our way through the North Star. Do not overlook Shaheed Ibrahim Hadi! I am truly surprised about why they do not put up pictures of Shaheed Ibrahim Hadi in gyms across the country! Of course, I humbly kiss the pure graves of the martyrs who used to attend the gym, but Shaheed Ibrahim Hadi differs from the rest. Why should they put his photo up now? Because even his name is effective in this environment. While he was living, he was a prominent spiritual personality and now that he has been martyred, it makes him even greater!

His father had a special love for him from amongst his children and would say, "This child has a different spiritual feeling. This child of mine will make my name known in the future," and I want to say to that great father that we have only begun to familiarise ourselves with Shaheed Ibrahim Hadi. He was a chivalrous athlete, and a person with the physique of an athlete and of chivalrous nature will naturally attract the attention of other youth. Once, when he was coming to the gym with his athletic physique and rucksack, his friends said to him, "Two of the girls of our neighbourhood were following you and were speaking about you. You know how to win hearts over!" They say that from the next day onwards, he did not carry a sports rucksack anymore! He would put his uniform in a plastic bag, wear a baggy shirt which would slightly cover his legs and would wear baggy and old trousers. The youth of his neighbourhood would pity him and say, "Everyone wants to have a physique like you and wear clothes to show this off!" He said, "I don't want to become the cause of misguidance for other youth."

The religious headquarters and the youth who wish to do cultural work in their neighbourhood should take Shaheed Ibrahim Hadi as a unique role model and study the ways of this martyr. It is as if he was familiar with the methods of teaching and nurturing. According to the nature of a believer regarding which

Amir al-Mu'minin (a) said, "A believer's nature is advice,"[2] he knew how to attract everyone. Many stories have been narrated about how he changed the youth and helped them move from this point to another point in their lives, from debauchery to presence on the warfront. He was even able to change the Iraqis who were against him and were shooting towards him from their trenches, make them surrender and make them change sides. One morning in one of the critical stages of the war, he decided to recite the adhan. They all said to him, "What has gotten into you that you want to recite the adhan now?" but he did not explain his reason to anyone and started to recite the adhan loudly. They were shooting towards him whilst he was reciting the adhan and one of the bullets struck him in the neck. Everyone asked, "Why did you do this?" They then took him into the trenches, and they did first aid on him while blood was flowing from his body. After a short while, they saw the Iraqis holding up a white flag, coming towards them. At first, they thought that it may be a trick of the enemy and therefore, they readied their weapons, but they later saw that the Iraqis had surrendered along with their commander. They asked, "Why did you surrender?" and the Iraqis replied, "Where is the one who recited the adhan?" They replied, "He was one of our soldiers whom you shot." They stated, "We surrendered because of his adhan," and they explained their story. This is the effect of a young athlete who would always be in the ring of the gym.

He was a champion of wrestling when he was in high school and said, "I was always careful during wrestling to never lay a finger upon the weak spot of my opponent while the tradition in wrestling is to throw the opponent to the ground using their weak spots." This shows that Ibrahim Hadi was truly a great champion. Shaheed Hadi was also witty and was unequalled in his bravery. The culture of our society is mostly in the hands of secular elements; otherwise, the whole world would know who Shaheed

---

2   Ghurar al-Hikam, saying. 1305

Ibrahim Hadi was. The cultural directors were not tactful enough nor were they able to make cultural advancements during these thirty-five years, otherwise even our children in primary school would recognise Shaheed Ibrahim Hadi. If a serial is created about Shaheed Ibrahim Hadi and this same martyr gives his blessing to the producer of this serial, I am sure that every year, the people would spend their Ramadan nights watching the serial of Shaheed Ibrahim Hadi. Shaheed Ibrahim Hadi was wounded several times in the flank and was also wounded in the face and the neck. This respected martyr has attractive stories filled with action, and the stories of the Western war films do not even compare to these stories. I have seen many war and action films from both the East and the West, but many of them are stories. If you read this book, you will surely lose interest in the stories they show you which are lies. I say to the respected filmmakers: If you are unaccomplished, come and work for Shaheed Ibrahim Hadi and you will become accomplished. He will make you accomplished himself. His stories will teach you the tactics of filmmaking. Go to him as he was himself; he was overly sincere.

Amongst the prominent characteristics of Ibrahim Hadi, if I wish to speak of one of his great characteristics, I must speak of his sincerity which was the main theme throughout his life. He would make sure that his actions would be in the way of Allah. This was his slogan and he would say, *"An action which is insincere has no use."* Imam Khomeini (ra) was someone who had this characteristic as a political leader to cultivate such flowers from the heart of this land and to discover such jewels from this society and nurture them. Some of the politicians are like Imam Khomeini (ra) in a way that when they look at the society, they bring the good people and the jewels out from the sea and make them role models for history, and there are also some politicians who, when they lead a society, they bring the crabs and eels out from that sea and they secure their power by relying on the riff-raff. Imam Khomeini (ra) and the Supreme Leader are two of the politicians who we have seen in contemporary times who brought Ibrahim Hadi out from the heart of our society. Currently, the Supreme Leader is not only highlighting these people from our society, but he is also highlighting them from our country. This is the light and outcome of wilayah, but some politicians search for their own people when they become active and infiltrate into society, like those people who brought the riff-raff from the outskirts of Madinah and set fire to the door of Ali (a)'s house. Ali (a) brought Miqdad, Ammar and Abu Zar with him, but who have they brought?! We want politicians who extract shining jewels like Shaheed Ibrahim Hadi from the heart of this land which is full of jewels. I would like to recite the poem of 'O' Iran, O' land full of jewels...' in the gatherings to honour Shaheed Ibrahim Hadi and martyrs like him. At that time, man will take pride. By reading this book, all the hidden beauties of this land have once again come alive for me.

I propagate one book: the book 'Peace be upon Ibrahim'.

The honoured compiler of the book writes, "When I completed the book, I didn't know how to do an istikharah, but I opened the Qur'an and made an intention and said, "O' Allah, what shall I name the book?" At the top of the page, it was written, 'Peace be upon Ibrahim.'[3] I suggest for the youth who are much into entertainment to read this book for them to see that you can also enjoy halal entertainment. This book isn't about a person who was only religious on the outside or claimed to be a revolutionary. After reading a few pages of this book, you will understand that Shaheed Hadi was not one of these people. By reading this book, you will witness a responsible person up close. I am sure that those who do not follow our religion and do not know our religion at all will respect our religion when they get to know Ibrahim Hadi and they

---

3   Saffat: 109

will tell us that we are lucky!"

THE ROLE MODEL

Despite its simplicity, Shaheed Ibrahim Hadi's personality had broad and affective dimensions. We say with courage that if many volumes of books, films and serials are produced about his characteristics, there would still be a need for more. This youth is a suitable role model for anyone with any kind of attitude to benefit from him. During his twenty-five-year presence in the material world, he taught mankind how to live, serve [Allah] and travel on His path correctly. His stories are beneficial for athletes, the defenders of the Islamic Revolution, reciters, teachers, coaches, and everyone who wishes to obey Allah's commands.

Ibrahim did not have a written will, but in the stories narrated about him, there are deeply hidden lessons which are effective in awakening the ignorant conscience. The book *'Peace be upon Ibrahim'* has been welcomed by those who wish to correct their worldly affairs and the affairs of the Hereafter and those who were after a correct role model, but seven years after printing the first book of *'Peace be upon Ibrahim'*, stories have come to us from here and there which were compelling, stories which we weren't able to gather for the first book despite our greatest efforts. We intended to add these stories to the first book, but the organisation did not agree as the book was already full. After the people of the community became familiar with this martyr, we received many donations. This book was propagated by the media and was even propagated by Seda-va-Seema.[4] They also told us many times to share our views on the book.

Therefore, we decided to prepare the second book and some of the divine guidance we received from this great personality has

---

4   The main media organisation in Iran

been mentioned at the end of the book. From the start of 2016, we were busy at work. We convinced some people who we did not interview for the first book to have an interview with us while some others expressed their willingness to have an interview. Like the first book, there were difficulties, difficulties which doubled the enjoyment of this work. We spent more than a month interviewing some of his friends and many times, we would constantly have to travel across Tehran. We travelled far and wide to be able to interview these people. We felt that it was important to do such a thing as people were eager to hear the rest of the stories from the life of someone who had a great effect on their lives. We had heard this from several people who were awaiting the rest of the stories. We increased our efforts so that we could complete the book faster, but in these years, we have witnessed Shaheed Ibrahim Hadi's blessings throughout the stages of our lives and in our work. The book was welcomed so warmly that at some times, even the directors were surprised!

The book *'Peace be upon Ibrahim'* was printed for the hundredth time [in Farsi]. By February 2017, on the anniversary of the martyrdom of the oppressed warriors of the Kumayl Trench, we had printed the book one hundred times and sold over five hundred thousand copies. It must be said that if we look at the books which the Supreme Leader has advised us to read, *'Peace be upon Ibrahim'* has broken the record of attracting the social audience. Until now, no book has been received with such a warm welcome. Of course, all this is with the divine blessings and without any help from the government or the media. When people from outside of Iran saw and heard Ibrahim's stories, they asked us if they could translate the book. In 2013, the book was translated into the language of Urdu and was sold in Kashmir and Pakistan. They were saying that this personality is influential for the Shias in our country. The students of Jamiatul Mustafa printed this book in the German language and was sold in the respective country. The work of translating it into Arabic is being done upon the suggestion of some Lebanese brothers, at the request of the Popular Mobilization Movement of Iraq and a few teachers from Khuzestan. This was all because Ibrahim sincerely acted in Allah's way and would not like it if he were praised, but Allah had other plans for him.

We are hopeful that Allah makes us firm and steadfast in Ibrahim's way and helps us achieve a good end in the way of martyrdom as part of the army of Mahdi, the awaited.

IN THE NAME OF OUR MOTHER

Narrator: The martyr's brother

Before Ibrahim was born, we moved house several times. We were tenants and like many of the people at that time, we did not live a comfortable life. I remember that we were tenants on Ajabgol Street for a while. Our landlady was a pious lady. She was a Qur'an teacher and would lecture in ladies' gatherings. Our mother's mannerisms became very spiritual when we lived in her house and she would pay a lot of importance to the Qur'an and duas. Our mother was a very practising and spiritual lady, but in that year, she had become even more spiritual.

Days passed until Ibrahim was born on the 21st of April and exactly on the 21st night of the holy month of Ramadan in that same house. Our mother and father loved him very much. He was a cute baby, but also very loving and loveable. The more time passed, the more our family would love Ibrahim. Everybody loved him and he was worthy of the love he received. Our father said several times, "All my children are good, but I love Ibrahim differently. You do not know that I pray for Ibrahim in my Salat ul-Layl from the depths of my heart. May Allah make him successful in this life and the next." Our mother felt the same way towards Ibrahim. Our mother's love for Ibrahim was to such an extent that she would do whatever Ibrahim said as soon as possible, but our mother was an experienced and understanding lady. Whenever any of our family or neighbours had a problem in their family life, they would ask for her advice. Our house had become a family court and our mother the judge. Whenever a person would tell our mother their problems, they would receive the best advice. Our mother always struggled so that the lives of the youth wouldn't be torn apart. I have seen many families that were saved from an ill fate by our mother's advice. Ibrahim was nothing less than our mother. He had heard our mother's words and advice and therefore, he started to mediate for some families. Even though I objected to this and would tell him, "These people are older than you and you are single, why do you get involved?" he continued doing his work.

One of the men from our neighbourhood got married to the daughter of one of the businessmen in the bazaar. The father of the bride was one of Ibrahim's friends. A short while after their marriage, shouting and fighting could be heard from their house from the street. It reached such a stage that they started to fight in the middle of the street and ruined their reputation. A few people got involved and broke up the fight, but everyone was saying, "These two have to get divorced. They are not compatible at all." Their lives continued separately until one day, Ibrahim went to meet the husband. Everybody in the neighbourhood knew Ibrahim as a believing and God-wary athlete. Ibrahim, who was friends with the wife's father, did not want the marriage to end in divorce. They sat on the steps next to our house and Ibrahim spoke with him for hours. Even though the husband was older than Ibrahim, he was sitting calmly and listening. An hour later, Ibrahim came into the house and ran to our mother, telling her what he said. Ibrahim asked our mother, "What shall I say now? The husband has accepted what I said." Our mother then told Ibrahim what the husband must be reminded of. Our mother went to the wife after Ibrahim insisted and they spoke with each other a few times. Ibrahim also carried out our mother's advice to the letter. The husband, who lived on our street, accepted Ibrahim's words and did what he advised him to do. Even though many of his friends and I told Ibrahim not to get involved, the sincerity in Ibrahim's words bore fruit. The husband and wife reconciled and started living together. A few years later when Ibrahim set off for the frontlines, they had children. They have a good life, many sons-in-law and several grandchildren. They believe that they owe their life to Ibrahim. Ibrahim's actions were the epitome of our master Ali (a)'s luminous words in which he said in Nahj al-Balaghah, letter forty-seven, "Mediating between Muslims is greater than any (recommended) prayers and fasts."

Ibrahim was on the warfront and our mother was constantly worried. Our mother was unbelievably happy whenever Ibrahim would come back on leave. Perhaps one could say that our mother died from the pain of separation from Ibrahim. It is impossible to describe our mother's condition when the news of Ibrahim's martyrdom was broadcasted and there was no news regarding the return of his body. Haj Hosein Allah-Karam came with the soldiers from the Intelligence Department and confirmed the news of Ibrahim's martyrdom, but every day, someone else would come and give us different information. One would say, "They have heard his voice on the Iraqi radio, and he is alive," while another said, "He has been martyred, the soldiers saw him," until we carried out a memorial service for him. After the gathering, just when our mother had accepted that her son had been martyred, a person came and said that Ibrahim was alive. He then said, "I want to bring an Ouija board for him so that I can tell whether he is alive or not with the help of the djinns." The day after, he came overjoyed and said, "Ma'am, I have good news, the Ouija board said that Ibrahim is alive!" Perhaps we can say that this news hurt our mother more than the news of his martyrdom. Our mother was burning on the inside. She would sit in front of Ibrahim's photo and cry bitterly. When Ibrahim didn't return after the return of the POWs, she fell ill. It reached such an extent that she would go to the freezer and eat ice! She would say, "My heart is burning! I want to cool down a little."

I went to my mother's house in November 1993. Her heart was hurting so I insisted on taking her to the hospital and she was taken into accident and emergency. The doctor examined her. She wasn't very ill, so I sat outside the ward. I was waiting for the doctor to discharge her as this had happened several times in the past, but one or two hours later, the doctor came for me and offered his condolences. I asked, "What? Are you sure you aren't making a mistake? My mother isn't ill." I ran to her bedside and she was lying down calmly and quietly. She couldn't bear to be separated from Ibrahim any longer and she joined her son.

A SERVANT OF ALLAH
Narrator: Abbas Hadi

We lived in a small house on Tajalli Road off Ajabgol Street. After years of being tenants, our father finally bought the house and we were saved from tenancy. Ibrahim started doing *Varzesh-e Bastani* with our father and brother in that house. Ibrahim founded a religious organisation in that house and encouraged many of the youth to attend these kinds of gatherings in this manner. Our home had two elaborate rooms and wasn't very spacious, but we would still hold *majalis* for Imam Husayn (a) in our house. One of the great things our father would do was that he would normally put a lamp up outside the door of our house to illuminate the dark street even though it would be stolen at least once a week. Another of our father's great characteristics was that he would say, "Leave the door of our house open from morning until the evening so that if someone, possibly a neighbour, needs or wants something, they can easily ask us."

One night, we left the door of our house open while we were eating our dinner. When we finished eating our dinner, as we were gathering the dishes, someone entered and called out, *'Ya Allah!'*[5] Our mother quickly put on her *chador*[6] and our father, who was sitting beside the *samovar*[7], told the person to come in. I asked my father who it was, and he said, "A servant of Allah, I don't know who." The man came into our courtyard and he asked if the gathering had ended. Our father replied, "Come and sit, let me pour you some tea." The poor man thought that the religious gathering had only recently ended. He sat next to our father and took the tea from his hands. He then looked at us and when he noticed that the boys were wearing their pyjamas and our mother was wearing a colourful chador, he realised what had happened. He became very embarrassed, but our father welcomed him warmly. The man drank the tea as quickly as he could, apologised and left. Ibrahim asked, "Did you know that man?" My father replied, "No, my dear, it was a blessing that a person came to our house, drank a cup of tea for the love of Imam Husayn (a) and left."

Although our father's financial situation was dire, he was an amiable and benevolent man. He would spend as much as he could in the way of Imam Husayn (a) and he even volunteered for the Ali Asghar (a) Religious Organisation. These morals and great *akhlaq* came together to give him good and righteous children. Ibrahim was in the former years of high school when he suffered the pain of becoming an orphan. Our father lived for almost sixty years and passed away in 1973.

---

5 A phrase generally used in the Eastern countries to alert inhabitants that you have entered
6 The traditional Islamic veil
7 A water boiler used normally to make tea in the Middle Eastern countries and Russia

VOLLEYBALL

Narrator: Mahdi Mohammadi

I was in the first year of high school at Karim Zand Khan High School. In my school, there were different types of students. At that time, there were six years of middle school and six years of high school, meaning that we had students ranging from the ages of 12 to 19. I remember that some of the students would drive and after school, they would work as taxi drivers. Some were even addicted to drugs. I was scared to make friends with anyone in my school until Allah decreed for me to meet one of His most sincere servants, someone unlike anyone I knew.

One day during physical education, I played volleyball with the older students. I tried to show the teacher how talented I was so that I could be chosen for the school volleyball team, but there was no space left on the team as the older students were taller and had larger physiques than me. One day when I was in class, the teacher was reading out the names of the students who were chosen for the team and I was sad that I wasn't chosen. Ibrahim, one of the stronger players on the school volleyball team, saw me and said, "Don't forget to come to practice this afternoon." I told him that I hadn't been chosen, but he replied, "It doesn't matter, come for practice." He then spoke with the teacher and praised my abilities. I went with Ibrahim after he kept insisting that I come. Many of them mocked me as I was small and had taken a space in the team, but Ibrahim was constantly passing to me throughout training and was encouraging me.

The next day in school and at break times, I would constantly look for him. He was my only friend. He would speak to me and I enjoyed the company. I noticed that all the students in the school respected him. He was so respectable that even the schoolteachers would observe certain *akhlaq* when they saw him. The day after, when I wanted to go to training from school, Ibrahim spoke to me for a little while and said, "Agha Mahdi, the athletic environment is spiritual. Try to make your actions and even your exercise to be in the way of Allah. If you haven't prayed or if you have to take an obligatory shower, first go and clean yourself." I said, "No Ibrahim, I prayed in the morning. I pay attention to these affairs. After training, I also pray again." Ibrahim said, "Then try to pray your Dhuhr on time. Tomorrow, let's pray congregational prayers in the mosque before we go to the training hall," and I agreed. He was so beloved to me that I would agree with whatever he said.

My friendship with Ibrahim became closer day by day. I was in the first year of high school and he was in his fourth. As well as playing and training with me, he would indirectly advise me. He would say, "Be careful of who you make friends with, be careful not to take anyone's rights. Make sure you don't oppress others," etc. A while later in the training hall, a few famous athletes came to our school while we were training. One of them was more famous than the rest. He was a footballer, but he would also play volleyball. He was Ali Parvin, one of the youths from our neighbourhood. He came with Reza Z. who was also one of the most famous volleyball players. Many others had also come to the hall to see them. There was a very nice atmosphere in the hall. I don't know who told them about Ibrahim's talents, but they suggested to them to play against him one on three. Ibrahim stood on one side and the other three stood opposite him. The children who came to watch the volleyball were all cheering Ibrahim on. The level of noise in the hall was deafening. Eventually, Ibrahim managed to beat them! I remember that Ali Parvin looked at him astounded.

Days passed until one afternoon, Ibrahim said to me in school, "Come, let's play volleyball one-on-one." We started to play and most of the children in my class had gathered around the field. Ibrahim was serving lightly so that I could return them. I was also trying hard so that I wouldn't lose to him even though I had seen him play against a few people and beat them. That day, I beat Ibrahim. Ibrahim played so badly that a child younger than him managed to beat him. You don't know how delighted I was in front of my classmates and I can still taste the sweetness of those moments, but Ibrahim was happy because he had made me happy.

THE FIGHT
Narrator: Sayyid Mohsen Mortazavi

The condition of the youth in our neighbourhood was becoming worse day by day. We would see them groups of youth going to the bar or nightclub every evening. Every day, these centres of corruption were increasing in the south of Tehran. The religious and faithful people were decreasing in number day by day and corrupt and drunk youth would take their place. We witnessed these conditions worsen in our neighbourhood. Despite being brought up in a large and religious family, I would see these youth in the street and neighbourhood when I reached the age of maturity. I had no doubt that these waves of corruption would eventually take me with them.

I had been attending Haj Hasan Najjar's gym for a little while and my arms had become stronger. One day, I noticed the youths living at the end of my street bothering some girls. For this reason, I approached them with my friends, Mahdi Hasan Qummi and (Shaheed) Sayyid Jawad Majdpour and a fight ensued. Although he had a small physique, Mahdi had brought a small dagger with him. He started to shout and the situation became volatile. Before the fight could begin properly, a few people came and calmed the situation. That was the day I first met Ibrahim Hadi. Ibrahim and Mahdi were friends and he knew me as well, but I had never met him. From that fight, a friendship blossomed between me and the youths at the end of our street. After the fight ended, Ibrahim looked at me and asked with a smile, "What do you work as, what do you do when you are bored?" I replied, "I spend the day working at the bazaar and at night I go to the gym. If you want, you can come with us to Haj Hasan Najjar's gym, next to the Salman Mosque, it's close." Ibrahim agreed. "Insha'Allah I will come tonight," he said.

That night, I left earlier and got ready. Of course, I was new to this environment. I thought to myself, "Wait until Ibrahim comes, and he realises I'm a weightlifter. I could have held my own in the fight." A few minutes after the exercise began, Ibrahim came with his friends. When he came in, Haj Hasan got up and said, "Agha Ibrahim Hadi! Welcome, champion, it's been a while!" I was surprised. I wanted to look good in front of Ibrahim, but apparently, he was a complete athlete! That night, my friends told me that Ibrahim was currently attending Agha Sheergeer's wrestling gym and is one of the weightlifters and wrestlers there. In conclusion, I was very embarrassed. I never imagined that the fight that day could be the foundation for a friendship. A short while later, I realised that he and I were spending day and night together. Ibrahim had become my whole life. Ibrahim was two years older than me. He would look after me and the others like an older brother. He would pay attention to where I would go and who I would go with. I can say confidently that, even though I was brought up in a large and religious family, I don't know how I would have turned out if Ibrahim wasn't looking out for me. I have no doubt that if Allah didn't put Ibrahim in my path, the corruption which took the youth of that time would have also destroyed me.

Allow me to explain clearly. Ibrahim dedicated his whole essence to guiding people like me. I would work at the bazaar from morning until afternoon. I would pray Maghrib and Isha in the mosque and then go to the gym with Ibrahim and a few others. Some nights, we would exercise until midnight and I would be so tired that when I would get home, I would fall asleep immediately. Therefore, there was no opportunity for me to socialise with my corrupt friends in the neighbourhood. Ibrahim made us busy in this manner. During the holidays, we would go to the mountains and sometimes, we would walk to Imamzadeh Dawud. He was a complete role model of *akhlaq* for us. I still remember the advice he would give me. He would tell us things that all youth should know. Those were such beautiful times. In the worst time to be alive, Allah put the best of His servants in my path, people like Ibrahim and Haj Hasan Najjar. Days passed and I spend all my time with Ibrahim. He would teach us about magnanimity and generosity. We enjoyed going to the mosque and praying on time because of our friendship with Ibrahim. This was at a time when most of the youth would mock you if you would go to the mosque.

The Islamic Unity Religious Organisation was founded. Ibrahim would recite for us and established a relationship between us and the Ahlulbayt (ams). Slowly, the youth developed a revolutionary passion within themselves. The late Imam Khomeini (ra) brought many towards Allah and spirituality, but according to all his friends, Ibrahim was a believing and revolutionary youth years before the Revolution. As well as spirituality, Ibrahim also taught us *akhlaq* and even how to interact with people. I remember there was a gym in a Moshiriyeh which was run by a seventy-year-old man. One night, the youth suggested that we go there to exercise, and we set off on a few motorcycles. When we went, we expected to be treated like guests like they would in other gyms, but not only did they not give us any space, they didn't even allow us to exercise! The youth left, but not before being very disrespectful. Some even suggested, "Come, let's go back and fight with them!" but Ibrahim shouted, "What are you talking about?! If anyone goes back, they have to deal with me!" The next day, I saw the owner of the Moshiriyeh gym at the bazaar. I went to him, said salaam and apologised to him for our behaviour the night before. The old man replied, "I appreciate it, no problem, but all your friends were rude except that youth who had a long beard." He then started praising Ibrahim. Years after Ibrahim's martyrdom, I went to the old man's gym once again and noticed that they had put up a large photo of Ibrahim above the ring.

THE STATE OF THE GREAT

Narrator: Amir Monjar

I have been studying books about the state of the scholars and great religious personalities for a while. Reading about the spirituality and state of these religious role models is beautiful, but even more interesting is that throughout my life, I was accompanied by a friend who showed me this state in real life. Our house was a short distance away from Ibrahim's. Ibrahim and I were almost the same age and our mothers were related. This was why we would visit each other often when we were children. During the era of the Revolution, these visits became more frequent, but during the era of Holy Defence, I wasn't able to accompany and benefit from Ibrahim as much as I used to because of my responsibilities. I was friends with many of the martyrs and I have studied the lives of many of the commanders of the Holy Defence era from close. I worked with Commander Shaheed Mohammad Boroujerdi for a while, but I can say with confidence that Ibrahim was a different kind of person. We had witnessed many people who had internal revolutions and became religious when the Revolution succeeded, but Ibrahim was a special religious personality even before the Revolution. Not only did he ensure to perform the Mustahabbat[8]

---

8   The recommended acts of Islam

and abstain from the Makruhat[9], but his gentle and spiritual soul was also such that no one in our society can be compared to him.

Let me give you an example so that you can sense the purity of his essence. Before the Revolution, we were going somewhere with Ibrahim. We were walking quickly on the sidewalk near Khorasan Square, but suddenly, Ibrahim slowed down. I looked back and asked, "What happened, weren't you in a rush?" He continued walking slowly and he said to me while pointing forwards, "Let's walk slowly so that we don't walk past that man over there." I looked back to where Ibrahim was pointing. There was a disabled man in front of us who was dragging his leg on the floor and was walking slowly. Ibrahim said, "If we pass by him quickly, he may become upset that he isn't able to walk like us. Walk a little slower so that he doesn't become upset." I said, "Ibrahim, we have work to do, what are you talking about? Let's walk faster. Let's walk through this street so we don't have to pass this disabled man." Ibrahim accepted and we continued walking on the adjacent street. Whenever I think of this story, I think to myself that Ibrahim was a champion wrestler. He was so strong at the time, he was able to defeat the greatest wrestlers of his weight class in thirty seconds, but this very person had such a kind heart, he would pay attention to the minutest of matters. Even though he was in a rush, he wasn't even willing to hurt the feelings of a disabled man!

I never saw Ibrahim trying to enjoy himself as 'enjoyment' had another meaning for him. To him, enjoyment meant bringing joy to others. It reminds me of the saying of Imam Ali (a), "Lowly people take pleasure from food and great people take pleasure from feeding others." If he received any money, he would try to

---

9   The acts looked down upon in Islam

give it to others. He was content with very little, but he tried as much as he could to help others.

In a neighbourhood close to ours, there was an old man by the name of Amu Ezzat who owned a shop. He was a sportsman in his day and whenever we would go to his shop, he would talk to us about the gyms of old. Ibrahim would go to his shop on any pretext he could find and would buy general groceries from him. He would also take us with him so that the old man could at least earn an income. Sometime later, Amu Ezzat's shop closed down and we didn't know where he was. We didn't even know whether he was alive or dead. To tell you the truth, I wasn't bothered until one day, we were riding a motorcycle down Rey Street when Ibrahim shouted for me to stop. I brought the motorcycle to a halt and asked what had happened. Ibrahim jumped off and went to the pavement. He came back to me joyfully and said, "Amir, come, Amu Ezzat is here!" I got off the motorcycle and saw that Amu Ezzat the shopkeeper was sitting on the side of the pavement and had put out a weighing scale so that people could weigh themselves and in that way, he could earn some money. Ibrahim went forward and asked, "How did you end up here, champion? Why is your shop closed?" Amu Ezzat let out a deep sigh and said, "They took my shop from me. Who should a person trust when his own son takes his shop and puts it up for sale? What should he do?" He continued, "I was unemployed for a while. One of the people from the bazaar bought me this weighing scale so that I could make some money. Now I don't go home so that I don't have to look at my son. My daughter's house is nearby, I'll go to her house." Ibrahim was upset and said, "Amu, let me take you home, it's getting dark." We took Amu Ezzat to his daughter's house on our motorcycle. Amu Ezzat's daughter's financial situation was worse than his own. They were living in a thirty-metre house. Ibrahim asked me how much money I had on me and as I had recently received my salary, I gave a thousand and seven hundred toman to Ibrahim. This was a lot in the era before the Revolution. He put the money in Amu Ezzat's pocket. After a while, Amu Ezzat apologised for not knowing it was there! On the way back, I was thinking about how kind Ibrahim was and how little the world meant in his eyes. Making someone happy was important for him, and he gave the money back to me a little while later.

Ibrahim gave one month's worth of his salary to this old man and it wasn't important to him that he had worked for a whole month at the bazaar and bore hardship to earn this money. His actions were the personification of the words of Amir al-Mu'mineen (a). When he was describing one of his companions by the name of Uthman ibn Haneef, he said, "In the past, I had a brother in the way of Allah who was great in my eyes as the world was small in his." These words were the guide of Ibrahim's path and *akhlaq*. He was a great person as the world and its adornments were small in his eyes.

A GUIDE TOWARDS SAYYID ASH-SHUHADA (A)

Narrator: Sayyid Ali Shojaei

We spent our youth together. At that time, Ibrahim was working at the bazaar and in the afternoon, we would spend time together and go to the mosque. One day, I said to him, "Ibrahim, have you noticed how many of the youth in our neighbourhood have become corrupt? Many of them have started drinking alcohol and sinning." Ibrahim agreed with a nod of his head and replied, "Let's do something. Let's establish a religious organisation and gather the youth together." We spoke to a few others and we set the foundation for a religious organisation. Our first few gatherings were on Tuesdays at his house on Tajalli Road. It was a small house which had two elaborate bedrooms and a small courtyard. Ibrahim's respected father sat at the door, would distribute tea among the attendees and help the volunteers. We had a lecturer and after the lecture, Ibrahim and I would recite. At that time, Ibrahim was young but would recite well. He would recite the poems and cry, leaving an effect on those attending the gathering. At the end of the gathering, Ibrahim prepared dinner for his friends and slowly, some of those youth who were being pulled towards sinning started to attend our weekly gatherings. We named this organisation 'The Youth of Mahdi Religious Organisation'.

Due to an increase in the attendees, Ibrahim's house wasn't large enough anymore. At that time, we had forty regular attendees every week. We would hold the gatherings at our friends' houses. All our friends accepted Ibrahim as the director of the organisation. Whenever we had no lecturer, Ibrahim would talk about building a friendship with Sayyid ash-Shuhada (a) and other subjects. Our weekly gatherings had a great effect and many of our friends in the neighbourhood eventually started going to the gym or working instead of going after sin. Ibrahim tried to fill their time. I remember that in those days, we went to Mashhad with some of our friends. On this journey, I got to know Ibrahim better. He would recite the *ziyarah* for us in the shrine. Once we returned, I noticed that tears were flowing down his face. All I saw of Ibrahim in the shrine of Imam Rida (a) was his limitless love for the Ahlulbayt (ams).

Days and years passed, and the Islamic Revolution succeeded. The religious organisation which Ibrahim founded compounded with another more well-known religious organisation in our neighbourhood, and it continues to hold weekly gatherings. Many of those people who were polluted by the corruption surrounding them at that time were saved from those conditions by Allah and Ibrahim's help and became very religious. Some of these people were also martyred in the era of Holy Defence. Ibrahim was martyred, but the religious organisation remained in our neighbourhood as a reminder of Ibrahim. During the Holy Defence, I saw Ibrahim in my dream. He was in a beautiful garden and some of his friends were beside him. I went forward and said salaam. I wanted to speak and ask him what the fruits of attending these religious gatherings were. Before I could say anything, he came forward and said himself, "Sayyid Ali, when I was martyred and I fell to the ground, Aba Abdillah (a) came and hugged me."

MODESTY

Narrator: Hosein Jahanbakhsh

Once I got to know Ibrahim in high school, I was always with him. He and I would exercise and attend religious gatherings or go to the mosque together. He was a role model of practical *akhlaq* for all his friends and those who were the same age as him. I don't want to repeat the words of his other friends as everyone knows that Ibrahim was a perfect human being from all aspects, but a question arose in my mind. Why was Ibrahim so different from the others and why was he at the forefront of observing ethical and religious issues? A while later, I looked closer. In addition to a mother and father who were very successful in nurturing him correctly, there was another person in our neighbourhood who was very effective in shaping his personality. He was a person who lived close to their house and Khorasan Square, a champion by the name of Sayyid Abbas.

He was an educated and muscular man who loved Ibrahim a lot. He would take Ibrahim wherever he went. He would say, "I love this child's modesty and *akhlaq*." He would visit many gyms and they would all welcome him warmly. I also went to exercise with Sayyid Abbas a few times. On the route there and back, Sayyid Abbas would talk to us and advise us indirectly. Sayyid Abbas was an experienced and educated man and he had a divine view of the world. He taught us much of what he believed without ordering us. Allah had given Ibrahim a caring teacher, someone who would guide him well on the path of his life.

A while later, we were informed that Sayyid Abbas had started to teach the commandos in the royal military, but it didn't match his personality. He had a beard and was very religious. Ibrahim himself asked Sayyid Abbas very respectfully regarding this subject and Sayyid Abbas told him, "They wanted me to teach the commandos and I accepted on the condition that I wouldn't have to shorten my beard, I would be able to pray on time and have freedom in practising my religion." Years after when Ibrahim entered the world of wrestling, Sayyid Abbas passed away in a car crash. He was a good guide for Ibrahim while he was present. One of the most important issues that Sayyid Abbas would emphasise upon when talking to Ibrahim was modesty. He would say, "If someone is modest, there is hope in his salvation, but someone who isn't modest has no religion." After he heard this, Ibrahim would always wear baggy clothes and would never take his clothes off in front of others. We had seen Ibrahim play many sports. He was an expert of ping pong, volleyball and even football. Once while playing football on concrete, Ibrahim did a bicycle kick! This is how much power and strength he had in his body, but I can never remember a time when we went to the swimming pool together, and this was because he was modest. Maybe he did go swimming, but he never went with his friends. Regarding wrestling and the clothes that a wrestler wears, he would buy a singlet which would cover his whole body and would buy the longest one, and he wouldn't take his clothes off in front of others. He would normally wear his wrestling clothes underneath his normal clothes at home and he would take off his outer clothes once he reached the hall.

This modesty was seen in every stage of Ibrahim's life. He had great modesty when he was around *non-mahram* women. When we would go to Ibrahim's house, we would never talk to his mother or sister. We would witness this modesty both in himself and his family. He would only choose modest people to become friends with. If he saw that someone was impudent or immodest, he would try to change that person's *akhlaq*. I even believe that he didn't want his body to return because of this very modesty. We went to the funeral of one of the martyrs in Behesht-e Zahra. When we were there, they bathed the martyr's body while people were watching. Ibrahim said, "I hope we don't become like this! If someone who bathes people's corpses isn't paying full attention, he may make a terrible mistake!" He then continued, "I have asked Allah for my body to be lost like the mother of the Imams, Sayyidah Fatimah (a), and therefore, my body wouldn't have to be bathed." For this reason, the poet says in his praise:

> *Being lost at war is in the essence of Ibrahim,*
> *It is itself a portion of the life of Ibrahim,*
> *Awareness, heroism, and kindness,*
> *Just an iota of the characteristics of Ibrahim!*

THE SLAP

Narrator: Mohammad Akbari Dulabi

It was the start of the 70s and we were teenagers. I would spend my days working at a light shop near the Chehel-Tan Shrine. When I had free time, I would hang out with my friends and play with my pigeons. At that time, many of the youths who were the same age as me were either polluted by the corruption of the times or busy working. I would come to Ajabgol Street with some of my friends in the afternoons. One time when I was playing there, I met someone the same age as me who seemed more spiritual than the others. He would speak, laugh, and joke with us, but he would never even talk about sin. His name was Ibrahim Hadi. I was glad as he was different from my other friends. He was a wrestler and had a strong body. At that time, I had many friends who were martyred later. Before and after that time, I had met at least fifty martyrs, but I can say that Ibrahim shines among them like a star for a thousand different reasons.

Let me give you an example. We would gather every Friday afternoon and play handy dandy[10] on the benches in front of our school. It was very fun, and we would waste a lot of time like this. Ibrahim would encourage us to play so that we wouldn't think about sinning. He would never sin. He would take us to the mosque at prayer time. He would always praise Agha Kafi's lectures in Mahdiyyeh and say, "Let's go to Mahdiyyeh on Friday morning for Dua Nudbah."[11] and I would reply, "Don't be ridiculous, forget it!" I enjoyed Ibrahim's company and we would talk and laugh. When I received my salary at the end of the week, I would buy ice cream for all my friends. Ibrahim would get annoyed and say, "Make a financial programme for yourself. Why do you use your whole salary at once? Have something to fall back onto."

One night, we went to Musa ibn Ja'far Mosque. I looked at Ibrahim while he was praying and noticed that his eyes were closed. I told him that it was makruh to close his eyes during prayer, but Ibrahim replied, "It is allowed if it helps you to pay attention during your prayers. When I close my eyes, I feel like my full attention is on my prayers." Since he was a teenager, Ibrahim would put time aside not only for me but for all the children of the neighbourhood. Many of them started to attend the mosque regularly and became practising. Of course, those who didn't become practising went into business and weren't corrupted. Believe me, when adults

---

10   A child's game in which one child guesses in which closed hand another holds some small object.

11   A supplication which is to be read on Fridays, Eid al-Ghadir, Eid al-Fitr and Eid al-Adha.

would join our group, they wouldn't swear in Ibrahim's presence out of respect. His whole essence would remind us of Allah. For this reason, I know he was a true believer as it has been mentioned in the narrations, "A believer is the one whose presence reminds you of Allah." His whole *akhlaq* was a lesson for us.

He would never stray from justice and the truth. For example, one of our neighbours was a violent and troublesome person and would go to the same gym as Ibrahim. One day, he got into a fight in the gym and broke another person's tooth. This person took our neighbour to court. In the court, I asked the victim to forgive him, but he didn't. Our neighbour, the suspect, told me to quickly call Ibrahim Hadi. I went and convinced Ibrahim to come. When Ibrahim arrived, the victim and the suspect both stood in respect. The victim, whose tooth was broken, said to the judge, "If Ibrahim asks, I will forgive him because I love him." Our neighbour was overjoyed and said, "Thank God! Ibrahim dear, tell him to forgive me," but Ibrahim said in a very serious tone, "No, don't forgive him! This man must learn not to cause fights for no reason." Everyone asked Ibrahim to forgive the man, but he didn't agree. The victim left and they took the assailant to jail. After our neighbour had spent twenty-four hours in a cell, Ibrahim said, "Now go and forgive him. He has to learn some respect."

However, the story that still burns my heart after forty years and makes me cry is the story of the slap. One morning, I didn't feel like going to work so I met up with Ibrahim and started to talk to him. His company was delightful. His advice had a great effect on everyone and made people hopeful of life and work. An hour later, my boss, a far relative of mine, came to us on his motorcycle and growled, "Now you dare to skip work and meet up with friends?!" He got off his motorcycle and walked to us. He looked at Ibrahim, who he didn't know, and slapped him hard on the face. He then took me to our workplace, but when he slapped Ibrahim, I felt very bad. My boss wasn't a bad person, but he didn't know how kindly Ibrahim would put time aside for us. Ibrahim could have answered him properly with his strong body and knock him out, but he didn't react at all. I met Ibrahim many times after that day and talked to him, but he never spoke of that day. This made me even more embarrassed and my belief in him increased.

KEBAB AND RICE

Narrator: Mostafa Taqvaei

I was friends with Ibrahim and a few others in the neighbourhood and we would always spend time together. We would play volleyball and wrestle and we'd also go to the gym together. We would spend most of our time together. Ibrahim was the only one amongst us who would work and he was always at the bazaar. He was earning a salary, but most of our group didn't have much money. One day, Ibrahim invited us all to the restaurant. He ordered the best food for us and we all ate together. It was delicious, especially for some of our friends who didn't have much money and weren't able to eat this kind of food regularly. Ibrahim was happy to see us eating so eagerly. The week after, Ibrahim invited us to the same restaurant again, but I said, "No, it isn't right if you always-" He interrupted, "Mostafa's going to pay today." When we sat at the table, Ibrahim nudged my leg and gestured for me to take something. He put his hand beneath the table, put some money in my hand and signalled at me to pay for the food and not to say anything. The week after, Ibrahim invited us all to the restaurant and said, "Today, so-and-so is paying." A month later, he invited us again and someone else paid for food. This continued for months. We spent some of the happiest moments of our youth in that restaurant.

If we say these things to our children, they might not think anything of it. Nowadays, rice is cooked in their houses regularly and kebab and rice is an ordinary dish, but at that time, most of the people in the society suffered from severe poverty and people would live in great hardship. Food cooked with rice became common in houses later. At that time, restaurant food was indeed cheap, but the people didn't have much money either. The masses were impoverished and eating such food was almost impossible for them.

Days and years passed, and Ibrahim was martyred. One day, I met up with my friends from the neighbourhood and we started to speak about him. "Do you remember when Ibrahim would take us to the restaurant, and we would eat kebab and rice?" I asked. Everybody agreed, nodding their heads. My friends said, "May Allah bless Ibrahim, we really felt like eating kebab and rice in those days." I then said, "I have to admit something. That night when Ibrahim said I will be paying for the food, I had no money. Ibrahim gave me money from underneath the table and told me to pay." When I said this, I could see the surprise on my friends' faces. One of my other friends said, "Ibrahim did the same for me. That night when I was supposed to pay for the food, he put money in my pocket and told me not to say anything," and the others agreed. That night, we realised the food was being paid for by Ibrahim but we hadn't known the whole time.

GUIDANCE

Narrator: One of the martyr's friends

When we would meet up with Ibrahim, he would tell us stories about the champions of old and he saw spirituality, belief, and trust in Allah in these champions. We had fallen in love with Ibrahim's personality. At that time, corruption was widespread and many of those the same age as myself had fallen into sexual sins. Once, Ibrahim said, "There was once an ancient hero who wrestled with a tree! The people present witnessed that he was so powerful, he was able to wrest the tree from its roots." We were enchanted by his words. He continued, "One of the reasons he was able to do this was he didn't act upon his lust before marriage and didn't do anything that would ruin his sexual potency." He advised us to busy ourselves with work or exercise and to not speak to the opposite gender until we reach the age of marriage as it slowly leads to destruction.

Days passed. In 1975, I was seventeen years old and was in a secret relationship with one of the girls in our neighbourhood. In a quiet hour, I was speaking to that girl in the middle of the road. I wasn't paying attention while I was talking to her. Suddenly, I saw Ibrahim coming towards us from the end of the road. I went pale in the face. There was nothing I could do. I went to the wall and stood around a metre away from the girl. Ibrahim walked past us with his head down and said salaam to us. I replied to his salaam and didn't say anything else. The colour had drained from my face. Ibrahim neither stopped nor spoke and he carried on walking. You can't comprehend how stressed I was. I wouldn't have been this upset had he had hit me in the middle of the street. Believe me, I wouldn't have been this worried had my parents found out. He was my best friend and I would spend all day with him. He was my wrestling and volleyball teacher and he was the one who introduced me to the world of volleyball. All I had was from Ibrahim. I couldn't sleep that night. What would Ibrahim say if he saw me the next day? What if he didn't speak to me when we were with the others?! These thoughts were driving me crazy. That night was the longest night of my life.

When the sun rose, I went straight to Ibrahim's house and rang the doorbell. He came to the door and said salaam to me warmly as if nothing had happened! I stayed quiet and Ibrahim didn't say anything either. A few minutes passed, but I couldn't piece words together to form a sentence. I said, "Ibrahim, say something. Hit me in the face. Swear at me. Call me a stupid idiot and remind me of how much you advised me!" Ibrahim replied as if he hadn't heard or seen anything, "What are you talking about?" I said, "Didn't you see me and my girlfriend yesterday-" He interrupted me and said, "What are you talking about, why should I shout at you? Maybe you have decided to marry the girl, and I shouldn't be an obstacle to that." He then paused for a bit and continued, "You are still my good friend." I looked at him with surprise. I then bade farewell and went back home. I started pondering; Ibrahim's *akhlaq* contained many lessons. That day, I thought for hours. Finally, I made my decision at night.

I went to the girl's house and said, "Look, most of the boys who make friends with girls don't want to get married and have Satanic intentions. That girl won't have a good life either." I then gave an example of a few people and continued, "These people's lives have been ruined!" I further added, "If you want to have a good life in the future, don't do these things. Someone who is with a different partner every day will have trouble in married life tomorrow." I then bade farewell and said, "Don't speak about this [affair]. I'm never coming back." I went straight to Ibrahim's house and told him what had happened. I said, "I could have had any kind of relationship with this girl, but I went, told her these things and bade farewell to her forever. Insha'Allah, as long as Allah helps me, I shall never do this again." Ibrahim broke the silence and said, "Go and pray for your mother and father. If it wasn't for your mother's pure milk and your father's halal sustenance, be sure that you would never have done this."

AKHLAQ

Narrator: Amir Monjar

Commander (Shaheed) Abdollah Masgar was one of the brave soldiers who lived in our neighbourhood. He loved Ibrahim a lot. The only photo of Ibrahim in military uniform was of him wearing this martyr's shirt. Ibrahim wore his shirt as a blessing and took a photo with it on. One day when I was at my workplace, Ibrahim called me and asked, "Amir, Shaheed Abdollah Masgar's memorial ceremony is tonight, are you coming?" I said yes and he added, "Also, I need to speak to you after the ceremony."

After the ceremony, Ibrahim called me over and when I went into the street, I saw one or two of the youths from our neighbourhood who were Ibrahim's co-workers. Ibrahim introduced me to them and said, "The rumours that are circulating about Ayatollah Beheshti have caused doubts in these two youths' minds. I told them that it would be better for you to speak to them as you know more than me about this." I spoke with them, and I presented many reasons and pieces of evidence to remove their doubts. When I went back home, I was glad I was able to resolve the intellectual problems for the religious youth, but Ibrahim was even happier than me. He thanked me, saying, "You don't understand what a great thing you have done. I spoke to them a lot but as I am their co-worker, it didn't have an effect, but you spoke to them from another position and presented good reasoning to them."

The day after, Ibrahim asked me, "Amir, can you come with me to Naser Khosrow Street?" and I said I could. He got onto my motorcycle and we stopped outside one of the shops on the street. Ibrahim went inside the store and started to speak with the shopkeeper very respectfully like always. I was standing outside the store, but I could see that Ibrahim was speaking respectfully. Afterwards, Ibrahim left the store followed by the shopkeeper. They said goodbye to one another, and he got onto the motorcycle. On the way, I asked Ibrahim, "By the way, what did you need from there?" He replied, "Someone came to our neighbourhood yesterday and said, 'I am an employee at one of the shops on Naser Khosrow Street. My boss doesn't pay me and has fired me.' I took the address and told him that I would speak with his boss and Insha'Allah, I have resolved his problems." I replied, "Ibrahim, you can't do anything, leave it." Ibrahim continued, "One must do what he can for Allah's servants. I only spoke to his boss and I tried to speak to him with good morals and *akhlaq*. Alhamdulillah, Allah helped us, and this person's problems were resolved." Imam Kadhim (a) said, "Verily, the seal of your deed's acceptance is helping your brothers with their needs and doing good to them as much as you can. Otherwise, none of your deeds will be accepted."[12]

FRIENDSHIP

Narrator: Amir Monjar

Ibrahim abolished everything from his essence except humanity. He was a true human, a human who not only saw worship as servitude to Allah but also as obeying His commands. He obeyed Allah's commands and wasn't frightened of any kind of hardship or difficulty in His way. I saw many of my friends who were misguided by their friends. They ignored Allah's orders because of peer pressure. This subject was also addressed in the Qur'an when the inhabitants of the Hellfire will say, "I wish I had not become friends with so-and-so..." meaning that some friendships lead to the Hellfire, but friendship with Ibrahim prepared the foundations for his friends' guidance. The difference between Ibrahim and the others was that he would care for everyone in the neighbourhood, especially the youth. Guiding people was very important to him. If there was potential to guide someone to the path in any way possible, he would put all his effort into guiding him. He wouldn't

---

12 Bihar al-Anwar, vol. 75, p. 379

forget even one person who had been misguided, but rather, he would double his efforts to help the person return to the path of Allah.

It was interesting to me to see how he would make friends with others. For example, a few of the youth from our neighbourhood would gather at the end of the road at night, light a fire in a large tin can and laugh loudly. They would make so much noise that it would start to bother the neighbours. It continued in this manner until one night, Ibrahim went to them, shook their hands with a smile and said salaam to them. One of the youth recognised Ibrahim, welcomed him and introduced him to the others, and Ibrahim spoke and laughed with them. He made friends with them this easily. He then told them that it was midnight and asked them to speak a little quieter. He continued doing this for the next few nights. He was trying to stop them from gathering at the end of the road and he was very successful at doing this. After that, he worked on them until they started to attend the mosque regularly.

One or two of his friends had different *akhlaq* and weren't religious. After the Revolution, Ibrahim tried to make them join the religious soldiers, but he wasn't able to. A short while later, they had a change of heart, and they wanted to go to the warfront, but no one accepted them. Ibrahim spoke with them continuously, encouraged them to join the military and asked them to pay attention to their religious issues more than ever. He then became their guarantor so they could join the military. They became believing and brave commanders and soldiers of the era of Holy Defence all due to Ibrahim's efforts.

One time when he was exercising in the gym, an ignorant group of people started a fight. Many people's reputations were ruined because of this knife fight. A short while later, Ibrahim bought many servings of kebab and rice and set up a gathering to mediate between the two groups. He put so much effort in that eventually, he was able to reconcile the two groups. The fruits of his efforts were seen much later when some of the youths who were bothering Ibrahim and Haj Hasan Najjar with their ignorance became righteous and believing people. They still live in our neighbourhood and believe that their guidance is a fruit of Ibrahim's efforts.

Ibrahim's brother narrates:

Two brothers in our neighbourhood were addicted to drugs. They had nobody to care for them which is what caused them to do these things. Ibrahim tried hard to make them abandon these drugs and eventually, he managed to do so. Once the Revolution succeeded, Ibrahim found them jobs and when the war began, he took them to the warfront. I complained to him, asking why he took them to the warfront, and he told me, "Actually, they are some of the best soldiers on the warfront. These people have stopped taking drugs. They shouldn't be left alone as they have nobody." Ibrahim continued, "I have even told my friends that if I am martyred, these two mustn't be left on their own. I told my friends to benefit from these brothers and not to leave them alone so that they can mingle with their drug addict friends again."

Ibrahim was martyred and those two brothers left the warfront. One day, they came to our house and cried for hours because they missed Ibrahim. They admitted that they were only alive and safe because of Ibrahim. Unfortunately, Ibrahim's friends left these two brothers to themselves for their own reasons and they didn't go back to the warfront. They stayed in the city and they started taking drugs again. A few years after the war, I was told that they had died.

IGNORANCE AND GUIDANCE

Narrator: Amir Monjar & one of Ibrahim's friends

Ibrahim would feel pity and would try to help those of his friends who were drowning in the Era of Oppressive Ignorance, but unfortunately, because of the bigotry of a group or neighbourhood and ethnic prejudices of some illiterate youths or sportsmen, fighting was rife amongst the youth.

Ibrahim had a friend called Mohammad whose culture and family differed from the rest of the people from our neighbourhood, but he trained with Ibrahim several times and even came to Haj Hasan's gym. He was a successful wrestler who trained at the Abu Muslim Gym. Just like everyone else, he fell in love with Ibrahim's personality the first time he met him.

Mohammad shined in the championships and was sent to the World Championship in Canada. Before leaving, Ibrahim invited him to Haj Hasan's gym. An hour after training, Ali Nasrollah and I went to the gym and as we were coming in, we heard Ibrahim shouting! He was yelling, "Hit me, but leave Mohammad alone! He's our guest!" When we entered, we saw three ignorant people carrying knives, looking for an opportunity to attack! Ibrahim was shouting and Mohammad was hiding behind him. When I entered, I took one of them down and took the knife out of his hand. Ali Nasrollah did the same and the last one fell on the floor when Ibrahim attacked him. They all scurried away when we defeated them. Muhammad bade farewell to Ibrahim and left. This Mohammad won the World Championships and he climbed the steps of progress until, in recent years, he became the head coach of the Iranian national Greco-wrestling team. He was Muhammad

Bana, one of our national heroes.

I asked some of my friends if they had seen him. I wanted to meet him himself and confirm the things I had heard people saying behind his back. I saw him at the mosque. I said salaam, asked him how he was and then asked, "Are you Mr so-and-so?" He nodded his head and asked me what I needed. I paused for a short while, looking at his face. You could see signs of ageing on his face, but he looked the same age as Ibrahim. His *akhlaq* was different from that which I had heard about him! I had heard that Ibrahim Hadi had organised documents for him to be released from prison many times. I had also heard that he was a rebellious person and would infuriate Ibrahim, but this person would pray on time and hadn't missed congregational prayers in a few years. He would even pray Fajr in congregation at the mosque. He worked as a gym coach and would train the youth of the neighbourhood as well. He was one of the religious people of the neighbourhood and was trusted by its inhabitants. For this reason, I didn't know where to start.

I said, "I want to speak to you about Ibrahim Hadi." He let out a deep sigh and said, "Ibrahim... You don't know what kind of an athlete he was. He was an expert at knockout blows and was unequalled. Once, in the competition hall, he won five fights with high scores and he defeated them all with knockout blows. Whenever I would take part in a fight, Ibrahim would stand next to the ring and guide me like a coach." I interrupted him and said, "I heard that Ibrahim struggled a lot to guide people like you and spent a lot of his time on you." His tone changed bitterly and his eyes welled up with tears. He paused a little then said, "God knows how much he struggled to guide me and those like me." He continued, "I would always get involved in fights because of the bad company I would keep. Of course, that's how the conditions of the times were. I was nothing less than my friends. I was sent to prison because of knife fights several times and Ibrahim signed my bail. I bothered him so much. He would come regardless of the weather, stand in front of my house in the Doulab neighbourhood and advise us. Most of his advice was about not fighting, but we were at the peak of youth and we were ignorant, and we didn't understand. Ibrahim put so much time aside for us so that we would change the way we lived our lives.

I will never forget the days of the Revolution. One day, he came to my house when it was raining heavily and spoke to me for a while about putting aside my knife, speaking to people kindly and not fighting, all while standing in the rain. Most of Ibrahim's advice to us was either about studying or going to work. I didn't work and for this reason, he started to search and got me a job at the newly established School of Arts. In conclusion, Ibrahim got me working before his martyrdom and left. Ibrahim left and eternal pain remained in our hearts." He paused for a bit to wipe away his tears and continued, "Ibrahim was sent by Allah to take our hands. I now work under one of the national wrestling champions and I teach the youth, but aside from work, I always speak to them about Ibrahim, about how to help people as well as wrestling and to try to be like Ibrahim, a true servant of Allah.

Of course, there were many like me, people whom Ibrahim put time aside for and were guided. Hamdollah Moradi was unequalled in 62-kilo wrestling. In the days building up to the Revolution, everyone was saying that he would be chosen for the national team, but he made friends with Ibrahim. He put wrestling aside, went to the warfront and was martyred. Qasim was another of our friends. He would always have a knife with him and fight a lot. He was also found by Ibrahim; I mean, Ibrahim's existential belief and allure also attracted him. His revolution was greater than mine. He went to the warfront with Ibrahim and ascended the stairs towards Allah one after the other. I heard that towards the end, he was appointed the commander of a battalion and was martyred. May Allah have mercy on all of them and let me join them. May Allah forgive our sins." He said these sentences and then he stood up. He bade farewell with teary eyes and a wounded heart and left.

THE WRESTLING GYM
Narrator: Ostad Sheergeer

I have had owned a gym in the south of Tehran in the Shaheed Ayatollah Sa'eedi Neighbourhood for over fifty years since the time there were only seven or eight gyms in the whole of Tehran. Most of our heroes were trained in these few gyms with limited equipment. At that time in this gym, we had both a ring and wrestling pads. We would work through hardship and with love and eagerness. May Allah forgive all those who have passed. I remember the coaches from that time well. Late Agha Gouderzi and Mohammadi went through a great amount of trouble to help the youth. We even prayed congregational prayers in a part of the ring. During these fifty years, I have seen all kinds of people in this environment, and in this very gym, world champions have been trained, from Mohammad Bana to others, but what was and is important for me is heroic *akhlaq*. I have made a schedule for all the wrestlers who have completed the foundation courses and written clear exercises for them.

Even though much time has passed, I still remember Ibrahim Hadi well. He would come here from the gym. I don't want to speak about him only because he was martyred. People know me, I don't do that. I have trained sportsmen who were martyred in the future. They were nothing special, but suddenly, their personality would change and they would leave for the warfront. However, Ibrahim had characteristics which made him stand out. After all these years, I still remember these characteristics well.

He wouldn't speak much. Contrary to many of the youth

of that time, he spoke modestly. Wrestling wasn't his goal. He had merely come to strengthen his body. He was always kind to all the sportsmen and would try to influence them. In the first few years when he started wrestling, he made friends with one of our wrestlers and spent a lot of time with him. After a while, this wrestler started to pray on time like Ibrahim. He had come to become a wrestling champion, but Ibrahim took him to the peak of heroism and pride. Later, he became one of the commanders of the military and the vice-commander of the Sayyid ash-Shuhada (a) Division. This capable wrestler was Shaheed Ja'far Jangravi, and Ibrahim changed the course of his life completely.

At that time when Ibrahim was training with us, he wasn't at the level of a national champion, but he would try a lot and practice well. He had a wonderful spiritual aura. Several times, I witnessed him letting his opponent defeat him in a competition! I complained to him about why he didn't adopt a certain strategy, but he would reply, "Well, this person had practised and struggled and also wanted to defeat his opponent." I would never understand what Ibrahim was talking about. Is it possible for someone to practice this much and then feel sympathy for his opponent during the competition?

He had a heroic mentality. I remember once while teaching wrestling strategies, the late Agha Gouderzi would speak about late Takhti and Tayyib and the other heroes of this land during the break. Ibrahim would listen more carefully than the others and would act upon his words. He learnt the path and culture of heroism. One of the other characteristics of Ibrahim which I had seen before in the late Takhti was that when competing, he would never target his opponent's weak spot. If he knew his opponent's left leg was hurting, he wouldn't go near it. Once, in a practice competition, Ibrahim was wrestling with someone the same weight as him. Ibrahim's opponent accidentally head-butted him in the face, causing his eye to swell and giving him a black eye. Ibrahim's opponent was frightened. He knew these kinds of things cause fights, but Ibrahim went forward and kissed his opponent on the forehead because he was a real hero. I found it strange that he would increase his opponent's morale by saying, "It's nothing, it happens during this sport. It's nothing to worry about." I had seen people act on the contrary many times before. The conclusion is that heroism had a different meaning to Ibrahim.

THE RIGHTS OF THE PEOPLE

Narrator: Mohammad Saeed Saleh-Taash

Our house was behind the training hall. I was in the same class as Abbas Hadi. A kind and respectable family lived next door to us who we used to visit, and we later learnt that the mother of this household was Abbas Hadi's aunt. My brother and I were twins and we made friends with Ibrahim through Abbas. Whenever we would meet him, he would come to us with a handful of pistachios and almonds and he would care for us a lot. Later, we realised that he was like that with everyone. Anyone who met him once would fall in love with his personality. I am now almost sixty years old and I am thankful to Allah that he placed one of His best servants in my path, especially during my youth. We understood what it meant to be good through Ibrahim. We understood the meaning of humanity through Ibrahim. My whole life was eclipsed by those few years. I lived with many of the martyrs from our neighbourhood. They were all great people, but they were incomparable to Ibrahim.

I remember that we went to the mountain with Ibrahim and I sprained my foot towards the beginning of our hike. Ibrahim carried me on his back, and we continued moving! You don't know how difficult and long the journey was. If it was anyone else, they would have said, "Stay here until I return," but he wanted to strengthen his legs and he didn't want to leave his friend behind. There is a valley close to Kulakchal Mountain which has a steep drop which would exhaust a person walking there even if they weren't carrying anything. Ibrahim carried me on his back on this route and took me up. On one hand, I was ashamed, but on the other, I was amazed by his physical strength. I have a friend by the name of Agha Fakhari who has a photo of Ibrahim in his shop. He had also experienced a similar interaction with Ibrahim to me. He was in love with Ibrahim's personality.

In conclusion, we had fallen in love with Ibrahim in such a way that my brother and I would only speak about him. Our parents also knew him, and they were glad that their sons were spending time with such a person. I say with courage that we learnt our religion and beliefs from Ibrahim. At about seventeen years old, he knew his religion better than his elders. One day, we were meant to play volleyball together, but I didn't have volleyball trainers. I said to one of Ibrahim's friends who was wearing some old trainers, "Give me your trainers so that I can play." I gave him my slippers and took his trainers and we started to play. After the game, I noticed that he had left so I went home. Less than an hour later, Ibrahim had come to our door, so I happily went to the door. I asked, "What are you doing?" He replied, "Saeed, Allah will forgive everything on the Day of Judgement except violating other people's rights. Be careful that you don't violate others' rights during your lifetime." He then continued, "Don't go near things that don't belong to you as much as you can and be very careful. If you borrow something from someone, make sure you give it back." I replied, "Agha Ibrahim, I am at your service. By the way, I don't know where your friend is, the one who I borrowed the trainers from because he left before the end of the game."

A MAN OF GOD
Narrator: Mahdi Hasan Qummi

We were living on Zeeba Street. My father worked as an ice-seller and after a few years of study, I also dropped out of school and started to work. My brothers would all work as well. While working on Zeeba Street, I saw a thin youth who was going to school with his head down, but I didn't speak to him until I went to the gym. I saw him on one of the first days I went to the gym, but I didn't know if he had previously been to the gym. The director of the gym invited him into the ring and said, "Ibrahim is the champion of Tehran's wrestling gyms." I liked him very much. He was a champion wrestler, but he was very calm and modest. Before entering the ring, he would shake hands with everybody, even with me, a teenage youth who had only recently joined the gym. Ibrahim greeted me more warmly than the others and from that day onwards, we were friends. I was happier than him as I had found a friend who was a complete compilation of all good and humanitarian characteristics. He addressed many issues for me regarding which people I should be friends with and which people I should stay away from in the first few days of our friendship. I still remember his advice. In the gym, we had people who, contrary to Ibrahim, were very indecent. Ibrahim described these people for me and said with the bad conditions of the society in mind, "Mahdi, make friends with someone weaker than you so that he cannot bother you." No one in my household would spend time with me and tell me what was right or wrong, but Ibrahim spent a lot of time with us and would advise us. Most of his advice was indirect and then he would try to take us with him to the mosque.

Towards the beginning, I wouldn't go to the mosque that often. When Ibrahim would go to make ablution, I would leave the mosque, but slowly, the allure of Ibrahim's personality made me a regular attendee of the mosque, meaning that I would go to the mosque out of love for Ibrahim.

Even though Ibrahim was only a youth, he would do strange things. One day, I came to the mosque. I was going to the bathroom, but I saw two youths come out and they told me, "The toilet is blocked so we'll go home to pray." I was about to go home, but at that moment, Ibrahim arrived. When he heard what had happened, he rolled up his sleeves, went to the bathroom and closed the door. Fifteen minutes later, he opened the door. The toilets were unblocked and the whole place was clean and tidy. He then went to wash his hands. Ibrahim was nothing in Allah's presence and he would do whatever he could to please Him. He saw himself as little in front of Allah and was humble in front of Him. Allah would also give him awesome greatness in the eyes of the people. As the poet says, "Learn humbleness if you are to search for bounty."

They say that a friend can either take one to heaven or hell, and this has also been addressed in the Qur'an, meaning that if many people are sent to the Hellfire, it is because of their friends. Along these years, I have seen people led to destruction by their irreligious friends and on the contrary, I have seen people led to heaven by friends like Ibrahim, and roads are now named after them [i.e. they were martyred]. The youth organisation was established in our neighbourhood. Ibrahim was one of the founders of this organisation, but he didn't accept any kind of position. Contrary to him, we were in love with position and responsibilities and therefore, he let us run the organisation. Ibrahim would recite very simply and without arrogance. Sometimes, a youth wanted to recite so Ibrahim would give the microphone to the youth halfway through his recitation and helped him so that the gathering would run smoothly. If he heard that there was another reciter at the gathering, he would not recite at any cost. His understanding of Imam Husayn (a)'s majlis was different from how we thought of it. I remember in Mostafa Taqvaei's house, Ibrahim wouldn't recite however much Mostafa's father insisted. He would insist and Ibrahim would reply, "Haj Abedi is here so I shall not recite."

In conclusion, however much we speak about Ibrahim's characteristics, it will still be little. My father, who had met all kinds of people, said to me, "Among your friends, there is one better than the rest, and that is Ibrahim Hadi. Listen to whatever he says." Even my brother who was irreligious approved of Ibrahim and didn't say anything contradicting his words. I say with courage that if Allah hadn't placed Ibrahim in my life, I don't know what my fate would've been. Not only me, but many of the youth of the neighbourhood wonder what fate would have awaited them had they not taken Ibrahim as their role model.

Ibrahim entered the arena of sport as he wanted to serve the servants of Allah. I heard Ibrahim say, "The day I decided to go into wrestling, my father advised me and said, 'Your aim for wrestling mustn't be to become a champion. Don't try to establish your position by breaking others. Try to help people with your sport.'" In conclusion, Allah placed Ibrahim in our lives so that we could witness a true human. Let me give another example so that you can witness another dimension of this man's personality. A drug addict lived on Zeeba Street and he would harass his family because of this addiction. Ibrahim tried very hard to make him stop, but he wasn't successful. He then spoke to him and asked, "Why do you harass your family?" He replied, "I have no choice. Every week, I use this much money on narcotics. If I have these drugs, I don't need them." Ibrahim gave him one year's worth of money for his drugs on the condition that he doesn't bother his family! For one year, his family and relatives lived in comfort. Ibrahim was then martyred, and the man told us this story. He died a short while after Ibrahim.

THE PATH OF ALLAH

Narrator: Mahdi Hasan Qummi

After his worship and servitude to Allah, Ibrahim's greatest characteristic was that he would try to guide and help people to the best of his capability. He wouldn't care about what others would say and what they were paying attention to. Sometimes, he would put himself in danger of being accused of sin when trying to guide others. I remember one day, we were at the Abu Muslim Gym. Ibrahim had learnt that a few of the sportsmen at the gym who were the same age as himself would go to the corrupt neighbourhoods of Tehran with a few of their older friends and engage in sin. They would disclose this information easily. Ibrahim talked to them a lot about this, but it had no effect. He eventually decided to go with them to guide everyone there! One day when we had finished exercising, he said to them very seriously, "Why are you leaving so quickly? At least take me with you once." They looked at each other surprised and agreed, so Ibrahim went with them! I was younger so I didn't go, but the afternoon the next day, I saw Ibrahim at the gym again, so I asked, "What's up, you went as well?!" Before beginning our exercises, he let out a deep sigh and said, "May Allah guide them all! On the way, I spoke a lot to these people, but their attention was focused on their older friend. This older friend of theirs was the source of their corruption." He then continued, "I never thought our friends could become so corrupt! They went to the corrupt neighbourhood of Gomrok without a second thought. I narrated a lot of sayings and recited Quranic verses for them, but they weren't paying attention. When their older friend, who had corrupted them all like himself, realised what I was doing, he shouted, 'Don't let this Ibrahim escape, and we'll take him with us by force!' I managed to run away before they grabbed me. They chased me, but they weren't able to catch me." I knew he was speaking the truth as he was the best racer I knew. He was very fast and agile. Ibrahim said ruefully, "I feel bad for these friends of ours. They're ruining their futures. Their parents are good, but these acts of haram prepare their destruction."

A while later, a youth came to the gym in very nice clothes and was watching. Ibrahim had something to do that day and left earlier than the others. When he left, two or three youths from that group went to that youth and they took him with them after making friends with him! I found this suspicious, so I quickly looked for Ibrahim, found him and told him what had happened. Ibrahim quickly borrowed his friend's bicycle and went to them. He found them near Ayatollah Sa'eedi Square and shouted at them to stop. He then took the youth aside and sent him home. Those three youth threatened him as well. The day after, Ibrahim thanked me and said, "Allah helped me to strengthen this body. It is in these circumstances that exercising and having a strong body show their benefits. If they weren't afraid of me, they would never have left that youth alone."

ENCOUNTERING EVIL

Narrator: Hosein Jahanbakhsh

Days passed and in the days leading up to the Revolution, no one had heard from Ibrahim for four days. Everyone was worried until he returned after the victory of the Revolution. When I asked him where he had been, he replied, "I was with my friends in the street clashes. I was with Javad Aradani when we were occupying the Ashratabad Base. Javad was the same weight as me and good sparring partner for me at the Abu Muslim Gym. He was a good person and his upper body was very muscular. During the fighting and shooting, a G3 bullet struck Javad in his left flank and came out of his right flank. After occupying the base, I took his body to the public hospital. At the public hospital, I witnessed that there were many martyrs whose bodies were mutilated and nobody dared to go near them and do the work for these martyrs. For this reason, I stayed and started to organise the conditions. Some bodies were burnt, some unidentified in which case, we had to do research and find their families. There was no one to do this." Ibrahim continued, "The Revolution had succeeded, and there was no fighting. We had to do something about this."

Ibrahim joined the revolutionary committee a few days after the Revolution succeeded. The committee's base was near Khorasan Square in Forutan Garage. The committee had a lot of manpower. Some committee bases would have a scholar who would issue religious verdicts. I had seen that they would whip people for drinking and transporting alcoholic beverages. One night close to Khorasan Square, they ordered a car to stop. The two youths in the car didn't pay any attention and drove faster. A little further on, Ibrahim bravely stopped the car, brought both passengers out of the car, and told them to open the boot of the car. We soon realised why they ran away; there was a box of twenty-four bottles of foreign alcoholic beverages in the boot. The two youths were shivering from fear. They were begging to not be reported. They feared the whip and for their reputation. Ibrahim looked at them and I was sure that he would behave with them in the best manner. I was waiting to see how he would act. Ibrahim picked up the box of alcohol and put it next to the gutter. He said to both, "There's only one way. Open each one of these and pour them into the gutter." They started. They opened each bottle of alcohol and poured them into the gutter. Ibrahim seized the opportunity and spoke to them about the evil of drinking. He told them the saying of the Holy Prophet (s), "Alcohol is the root of all evil and is one of the greatest sins." He told them that Allah wouldn't look at the drunkards mercifully and Imam Sadiq (a) said, "The drunkard will not enter heaven," and, "Every evil has a lock and alcohol is the key to all these locks." They were listening attentively and when they finished, Ibrahim concluded, "Islam has set these rules so that society can function properly, otherwise mine and your families wouldn't be able to travel in the streets freely." They showed their gratitude, bade farewell, and left. I had no doubt that this good *akhlaq* would show a result even against the purest of evil.

A few months after the success of the Revolution, Ibrahim and I were working with the committee unofficially whenever we had time. We had jobs in the Education Department, but we would also coordinate with the committee. One day, Ibrahim came to my house at noon and called me. I came to the door and invited him in, but he replied, "I have something to do. I only wanted some money for a good cause so don't expect the money back." We had an inside joke, so I looked at him and said laughing, "What's happened? Have you resorted to beggary?" He laughed and said, "If you have nothing to do, let's go together and you can see why I want the money." That day, I had one hundred tomans. He then left and gathered one hundred tomans from Mostafa, one hundred from Amir, one hundred from Saeed and so on. He gathered approximately one thousand tomans. We went to the Khorasan Committee and there was a youth who looked about twenty years old sitting at the door. Ibrahim asked, "Has your problem been resolved?" but the youth replied sadly, "No, what should I do?" Ibrahim went inside and came out a few minutes later with a large wooden box which contained a few cassettes. I realised that this youth was a door to door cassette seller and would sell illegal cassettes. Ibrahim took the youth aside and gave him the box. They had destroyed most of his cassettes. The youth looked inside the box and there were only a few cassettes left at the bottom of the box. His whole capital had been wasted and Ibrahim realised this from the look on his face. He said, "Look, my brother, a man must earn halal sustenance. You won't get anything from haram sustenance." He then asked, "How much of your capital has been wasted?" The youth replied, "About one hundred cassettes, each one costing five tomans." Ibrahim put his hand in his pocket and said, "This is one thousand tomans of halal wealth. Go and do business with this halal sustenance." The youth was so happy, he didn't know what to do with himself! He kissed Ibrahim's face.

As he was leaving, Ibrahim seized the opportunity and said, "My dear brother, all the scholars have said listening to the voice of a woman is haram. Haram music makes a person irreligious and the money which is earned from these tools of haram has no blessing. It is haram, don't go after these sorts of things. Ask Allah to help you." The youth replied, "Definitely. I swear to God that I believe in halal sustenance, but I didn't know that these cassettes were haram. I am at your service. I assure you that I won't do anything like that again." The youth threw the remaining cassettes in the bin and left. As he was leaving, he turned around and looked back at us. Ibrahim guided him with sincerity, and I was sure that this sincerity would leave an effect.

I remember reading once that a person went to Ayatollah Shahabadi, Imam Khomeini (ra)'s teacher, and said, "I do not enjoy praying and I enjoy some of my sins. Is there a praise of Allah I can recite to change this?" Ayatollah Shahabadi immediately asked, "Do you listen to haram music?" The person was scared and said yes. Ayatollah Shahabadi said, "Praising Allah isn't needed, but just stop listening to haram music. The haram voice of a person encourages people to sin, prevents him from praying and takes him to Satan."

THE TOYOTA
Narrator: Abbas Hadi

The Revolution had recently succeeded, and the war hadn't yet begun. Ibrahim was working in a governmental agency and I was also working as a guard for Seda-va-Seema for a short while. In those days, we were living on Zeeba Street, near Mohammadi Mosque. One day when I was standing at the end of our street, Ibrahim came back from work in the afternoon. This time, however, he had come in a very nice car! He parked his brand-new white Toyota in front of our house and got out. I was extremely surprised. I went up to him and exclaimed, "It's such a nice car! Where was it, how much did you buy it for?" Ibrahim locked the car and went to the house. I followed him into the house, and I started to describe his car to the family. then I said to him, "Give me the keys, let me drive around the block once." Ibrahim was silent and didn't say anything. A little while later, he said, "No, this car isn't good for us. I think we're going to fall off." I replied, "Don't you fall off a motorcycle?" but he repeated his words and said, "This car can make us fall off and can distance us from everything, from Allah and the people. I am going to give it to someone else tomorrow." I asked, "To who? Where did you get it in the first place?" He replied, "One of the scholars in the department gave this car to me as a gift, but I have no use for it." I said, "No problem, give it to me. At least if mum or one of the others want to go somewhere-" He interrupted, "No, it is useless."

The next day, he went to work without the car. In the afternoon, someone rang the doorbell so I went to the door. A man was standing at the door, so I said salaam and he replied likewise. He said while looking at the car, "I have come to take the keys to this car. This is Agha Hadi's house, have I come to the correct house?" I said, "Yes, who are you?" He replied, "Agha Ibrahim has sent me. You must be Agha Abbas." I was sure that he was telling the truth by the proof he gave me. I gave him the keys and he left with the car. That night, I spoke with Ibrahim a lot. I said things like what are you doing, why don't you keep a car for yourself, why do you give everything away, you also have a future and a family, but Ibrahim smiled like normal. He then said only one sentence, "It is good that this car has gone." He had faith in the things he would do. He knew that cutting off from the people and society and becoming comfortable in life started with these little things; first a classy car and then a large house and so on. The day after, he took the Volkswagen from Agha Hosein Jahanbakhsh, one of his friends, and parked it outside. He said, "This is your car. If you want to go anywhere, there is a car." I walked past the Volkswagen, distraught and went inside the house.

IN THE PRESENCE OF THE SCHOLARS

Narrator: Amir Monjar & others

I have seen many people who look religious with a rosary in their hands and are seeking repentance from Allah when leaving their houses, but some of these people only do apparent repentance and don't do anything for Allah. When they are presented the choice of sin, it isn't obvious to say that they will refrain from it. Ibrahim was a man of care and judgement. He would be careful of his actions and judge himself, but these issues did not affect his appearance i.e. around his friends and others, he was very ordinary and simple. He would speak, laugh, and joke with us. You would have had to meet Ibrahim to understand the sincerity in his actions and his judgement and care. He had attained this spirituality through attending the lessons of the scholars and the lecturers at the religious gatherings. He would always go to the mosque and benefit from the words of the great people.

Ibrahim didn't become a reciter overnight. He would always be the first to go to some people and ask them to help him serve the

Ahlulbayt (ams). Agha Torabi was one of these people. I went to his house with Ibrahim. Agha Torabi was one of the pioneering sincere reciters. Ibrahim sat in front of him humbly and said, "Haj Agha, I have come to ask you to help me serve Imam Husayn (a)." Agha Torabi loved Ibrahim very much and had taught him whatever styles of recitation and poems he knew.

Before the Revolution, Ibrahim's family moved to a new house on Zeeba Street, a street on which almost every house was illuminated by a great scholar. The Imam al-Qa'im Islamic Seminary, Mohammadi Mosque, and tens of Husayniyyahs[13] proved the worth of the faith of the people of this neighbourhood. A great scholar by the name of Allamah Mohammad Taqi Jafri lived in the same neighbourhood as Ibrahim. This great scholar had splendid *akhlaq* and many people from the neighbourhood admired him. Ibrahim was also one of his admirers and would attend the gatherings and meetings which would take place at his house. Allamah Jafri's son adored Ibrahim's personality and became one of his close friends. Ibrahim benefited from this great scholar and loved him very much, and this was a two-way relationship. Allamah Jafri loved Ibrahim as he was a revolutionary and believing youth. When Ibrahim was wounded in Operation Fath ol-Mobin, Allamah Jafri visited Ibrahim's house and stayed there for an hour, something which he wouldn't do very often! Ali Jafri, the son of the Allamah, said in an interview with some reporters, "When Ibrahim was wounded and they brought him home, Allamah asked us to take him to visit Ibrahim. When Ibrahim realised Allamah was in his house, he wanted to stand despite his wounds and said, 'My teacher, why did you put yourself out? We would have come to visit you when I recover.' Allamah replied, 'It is our duty to visit you. You have put your life on the line and today, it is our duty to visit you.' Allamah continued, 'You would always come and learn from us. Today, it's my turn to learn from you.' Ibrahim became very

---

13   Centers dedicated to commemorating Imam Husayn (a)

embarrassed and replied, 'Please sit, my teacher. I am the dust on your feet. Whatever I have is from you. Pray that I can be a soldier on the path of Wilayah.'"

Brother Ali Kaleej describes that day as follows, "As I was passing through Ayatollah Sa'eedi Street, a Land Rover horned at me. I looked back and saw one of my friends sitting at the wheel. He asked, 'Do you want to come and meet Agha Ibrahim?' I said yes and jumped in the car, but when I looked back, I felt very embarrassed. Allamah Mohammad Taqi Jafri was sitting right behind me! I said salaam to him respectfully. When we reached Ibrahim's house, after the traditional pleasantries, Ibrahim said, 'My teacher, on the frontline, many issues became clear to me." He then put his hands in the form of a bowl and said, "If the world is like this sphere, Imam Zaman (aj) surrounds the world like these hands of mine, and Allah is also witnessing and All-seeing over this world." Allamah was sitting in silence, pondering over Ibrahim's mystical interpretations. Ibrahim then went on to describe the miracles and unseen assistance he had witnessed.

Mohammad Khorsheedi, one of Ibrahim's neighbours and friends, said, "When Ibrahim was in Tehran because of his wounds, I took him to Zeeba Street on my motorcycle. I asked him where he was going. "I'm going to Allamah Jafri's house," he replied. I asked, "The Allamah who has a thick Turkish accent and speaks on TV? Can I come as well" He replied, "Yes, come, no problem." We went to Allamah Jafri's house. He was giving a speech, and a few people were sitting around him. Ibrahim entered the room assisted by a crutch. When the Allamah saw him, he got up and went to welcome Ibrahim. He then said in his beautiful accent, "Agha Ibrahim! Please sit, please!" He took Ibrahim to the front of the gathering and everyone stood in his respect. Allamah then said things which were so strange, if I wasn't there, I wouldn't believe it. "Agha Ibrahim, go and sit in my position," he insisted, "We must be your students." When Allamah said this sentence, I looked at Ibrahim's face. His face was as red as a beetroot. He sat right there next to the students and said, "My teacher, I beg you, don't embarrass me." After insisting, Allamah returned to his place, but before continuing his discussion, he turned to his students and said a sentence I will never forget, "This Agha Ibrahim is my teacher." I didn't know much about Allamah Jafri's intellectual status at that time and had only seen him speaking on TV, but I knew as much as to know that such words from a philosopher and a great scholar are not without reason."

Days passed until Ibrahim was martyred in Operation Before the Dawn. They didn't announce Ibrahim's martyrdom for a while. Some thought that he was still alive or was taken captive until they announced that he had been lost at war. The person who informed Allamah of this news says, "When Allamah Jafri heard that Ibrahim had been martyred and his body was lost at war, he became very upset. As soon as he heard the news, he looked at those around him and recited a couplet of poetry." Allamah said in one of his books, "The strongest people are those who are dominant over themselves even if they don't own anything in this world. On the contrary, if someone owns the whole world but is deprived of being dominant over his own soul, this person must be considered as the most unable person."[14]

THE PRACTICAL TRADITION

Narrator: Hojjat al-Islam Dr Sayyid Mohsen Meeri

In 1975, I started going to the Abu Muslim Gym under the management of Ostad Sheergeer. I enjoyed wrestling and I had heard there were good coaches and wrestlers in this gym. I heard

---

14 Allamah Mohammad Taqi Jafri, Imam Husayn (a): The Martyr of the Pioneer Culture of Mankind, p. 165

people say, "Ostad Sheergeer and Mohammadi pay more attention to spiritual and humanitarian characteristics." I joined this athletic environment and within the first few days, I got to know Ibrahim Hadi and his good *akhlaq* like many of the other athletes. I never wanted leave him and he influenced my *akhlaq*. We would spend all our time together. On the weekends and holidays, we would play volleyball on Khavaran Street, close to my father's garage. Days passed and I decided to attend Agha Mojtahedi's Hawzah. Ibrahim encouraged me a lot to do so.

Four decades have now passed and throughout these years, I have made many friends and met many coaches and people in university and the Hawzah. I am a lecturer at a university and a Hawzah teacher. I have been on many journeys for propagation inside and outside of the country but believe me when I tell you I still haven't been able to find another person who has all the same characteristics as Ibrahim!

I was younger than him, yet he always had my back. He would stand next to the wrestling cushions during the competitions and act as my coach. I was friends with him since then and we still have a strong friendship! He is still looking after me right now! In this past month, he has come to me twice in my dreams and helped me with my issues in life. The last time was just a few days ago when I wanted to do something. Ibrahim came, advised me like an older brother and said, "Don't do this for these reasons!" I can elaborate on Ibrahim's way of life or practical tradition from what I have learnt from the Hawzah and the scholars in the following manner:

The first subject is spiritual wayfaring. Some spiritual figures undertake the path of separating from the people, night vigil and praising Allah. They essentially refrain from all worldly affairs. They try to reach Allah in this manner. Others see the path of spiritual wayfaring through *ziyarah*. They distance themselves from the people of the world and travel to Karbala, Mashhad, Makkah, and other holy cities. Other spiritual figures study. They live their lives learning, researching, and reading books to reach

Allah. However, Ibrahim Hadi's way was different. He would live among the people and at the heart of society. He would care for, eat with and think like the people, especially the youth, but at the same time, he didn't pollute himself with the world. He used different techniques to infiltrate the heart of the listener and guide them to the path of Allah. These were exactly the same techniques used by the Holy Prophet (s) and the Ahlulbayt (ams). The Prophet of Allah (s) would live in the society and put all his effort into familiarising the listener with Allah.

The next subject is Ibrahim's social skills. I have seen very few people who are able to relate to everyone like Ibrahim could. At home, he was friends with his brothers and when he got to know me, he would talk to my father and brother as if he knew them for years. He would make friends with different people with different jobs. He would make friends with people who were both younger and older than him quickly. There were corrupt people in our neighbourhood who would talk about their inappropriate acts freely, but Ibrahim would be able to make friends with them. Of course, these social skills had a purpose. Everything Ibrahim did was for a specific purpose, and that purpose was always to guide people towards Allah. Sometimes, we would see a young boy who looked like he was in primary school go to Ibrahim's house and speak with him for hours on end! He had domestic problems and considered Ibrahim as his confidante. Ibrahim was loyal to his trust and spoke with him for hours until his problems were resolved. Sometimes, we would see when Ibrahim saw the other person wasn't turning towards the right path at all, he would cut off his relationship with this person. He would continue his friendship with those who at least had some humanity in themselves. If he realised that he wasn't able to guide them, he would either not establish a friendship with them or he would end it. For example, some gyms in our neighbourhood didn't care for values. Ibrahim tried to change them, but he wasn't able to and therefore, he stopped trying. In the days leading up to the Revolution, we witnessed the results of these friendships. Ibrahim had managed to train the most corrupt and unprincipled people to become the best soldiers for the Revolution. Every person who had made friends with Ibrahim became the best revolutionary and cultural soldier of their neighbourhood.

Ibrahim's next trait was his positive thinking. This was beneficial when meeting different people. It has been mentioned in the narrations that the highest level of faith is where one doesn't see anything lower than him/herself and that s/he pays attention to the positive aspects of the other person. Ibrahim followed this narration to the letter. If he made friends with somebody and others would reproach him for doing this, he would tell them about the person's good *akhlaq*, but he wouldn't tell them the negative aspects. I had never seen Ibrahim order someone to stop doing a certain sin. He wouldn't say anything, but he would do something which would make the person realise his mistake. Ibrahim acted exactly upon the following order of the Ahlulbayt (ams), "Invite people [to Allah's path] without your tongue.

Another topic that must be mentioned is showing off is common amongst the youth. They like to be the centre of attention and when they grow older, they want to find a job and maybe become a director. This is the nature of many people. Ibrahim hated showing off to others and would even do things so people wouldn't notice him! When the Revolution succeeded, Agha Davoudi, his friend and coach, became the director of the Sports Department. He suggested that Ibrahim join the organisation and accept a directorial post, but he didn't accept. I remember that Ibrahim loved being unknown and would like to do things without announcing them since that time, I mean before the Revolution. He was an accomplished wrestler, but he never wanted to become a champion nor did he ever join the national team. He never wanted position nor did he ever want to be noticed. For this reason, he is so well-known today. From that time, he was attached to the mother of the Imams (ams) and had heard that Lady Fatimah (a) was the most unknown of the Infallibles. She neither had a specified grave nor have the historians written much about her. There are very few sayings narrated from her, but Allah gave her such a position that the Imams (ams) would say, "We are Allah's witness over you, and our mother is Allah's witness over us."

The next topic of Ibrahim's personality was his wisdom. The word wisdom (Hikmah) has been used often in the science of understanding the Qur'an. Man must determine his position well and struggle in the way of Allah. They call these wise actions. Wisdom in its real meaning was personified in his *akhlaq* and actions. Ibrahim has no will or poem attributed to him, only one or two letters that were left behind by him, but he would act wisely and effectively, and a lot of people whom he managed to guide confirm this point.

Another of his characteristics was his coolness. He would never get angry when speaking to people. I can never recall Ibrahim getting into a fight. Ibrahim's behaviour was very calculated at a time when the youth would generally act rashly. If he saw one of his friends making a mistake, he wouldn't hang out with him for a while until he realised what he had done wrong.

Another of his traits was his dignity. He would act in such a way as if he had all the comforts of the world. As he was an orphan, he wasn't very well off, but he made a living for himself by working in the bazaar. He would also put some money aside for other people. He wouldn't get excited over good opportunities neither would he get upset over missed opportunities. These traits made him a firm character, but his last trait was his natural wit. He would joke and laugh when he would interact with others, and this added to the allure of his words and *akhlaq*. He would sometimes argue with his friends during volleyball and wrestling. He would always smile and for this reason, everyone would enjoy his company.

THE RELIGIOUS ORGANISATION

Narrator: Mohammad Saeed Salehtaash

At the start of the 70s, the conduct in the Zeeba Street neighbourhood had grown increasingly inappropriate. I had witnessed a neighbourhood with a religious background disgraced by the new generation of youth. Ibrahim Hadi moved to our neighbourhood in these conditions. They were living in Ibrahim's aunt's house, but this Ibrahim was different to the Ibrahim I knew a few years earlier. At that time, Ibrahim was a youth who loved volleyball, but now he was a complete wrestler. One day, the youth started talking about Ibrahim. One said, "Ibrahim is so sophisticated." Another said, "He is a champion and has no rival in wrestling," and another said, "He is so strong. No one can lift Ibrahim off the floor." Believe me, all the youth of our neighbourhood unknowingly loved Ibrahim. When he would go to the gym, I saw a large group of those same youth following him. I swear that Ibrahim's personality guided many misguided people to the right path. I saw youths who were always sinning and drinking alcohol leave their past because they made friends with Ibrahim. They were constantly looking for a new role model.

Abdollah Masgar was another of the youths who lived in our neighbourhood at that time. He had a bachelor's degree and was very warm and welcoming. He was an anti-monarchical political personality and was one of Ibrahim's best friends. One time when we were playing volleyball in the street, Abdollah came, said salaam and said, "Guys, we want to establish a religious organisation for the youth of the neighbourhood. Our aim for establishing this organisation isn't just to recite for Imam Husayn (a) and to recite the Qur'an, but rather, we want it to be a place where the youth of the neighbourhood can meet up with each other. We want to meet up at least every week." We all agreed, and we would meet up every week as per Abdollah Masgar's idea. You can't imagine how many blessings came from this organisation. Abdollah set up Qur'an classes for us, and many of the youth of the neighbourhood including myself learnt how to recite the Qur'an from this organisation. As he was the most knowledgeable out of all of us, Abdollah would speak about the interpretations of the verses and the current issues. The youth were so attached to this organisation that if they were on the other side of the city, they would come to our neighbourhood in time for the meetings. Ibrahim was a firm foundation for this organisation. Many of the youth would be encouraged to come to religious gatherings because they knew Ibrahim would be there. I remember during the days leading up to the Revolution, this religious organisation laid the foundation for the youth to get to know the Revolution and Imam Khomeini (ra).

The Revolution succeeded and the era of strife and Holy Defence began. When I looked closely, I noticed that most of the people who were once corrupt but had some hope of guidance were on the warfront with Ibrahim. Two of them were even martyred. Even though I had witnessed their spiritual awakenings, I thought to myself, "How can they go to heaven when they were like that in this world!?" That night, I saw those two people in my dream. They had a very great position in heaven. I was sure that these people were of those drawn close to Allah. Days passed and whenever Ibrahim would come back on leave, he would bring blessings to the group of our friends. Once, I saw in my dream that Ibrahim had come back on leave. I missed him a lot, so in the morning, I went to his house. My heart was in my mouth. I was thinking to myself, "You can't disturb people because of a dream." A few moments later, Ibrahim was standing at the doorstep! You can't imagine how happy I was. We hugged each other and he asked, "How did you know that I had come?" I replied, "I love you so much that whenever you come on leave, I see a dream." Even though he had limited time, we never forgot the memories of us playing volleyball together day and night. We would remember the stories and laugh.

I remember I saw him once before the last time he set off for the warfront. He said, "I am going, do you need anything?" He was sure that this would be our last meeting. We then started to remember our volleyball memories. Ibrahim paused and then continued, "I will go and prepare the ball and net [on the other side] and then you can come." He said that and left. Years passed and Allah blessed me with the ability to compose couplets about different subjects, but one of the first poems I composed was about Ibrahim. I wrote about him:

There is a passion in the window of our house,
As the passer-by of our street is a man of Allah,
Humble and generous, of a graceful gait,
Every step of his shows his love towards perfection and ascension,
He is the guide (Hadi) of love, pure and clean,
As if he was a narration and word from Allah,
The verses of Allah as if he threw light into their hearts,
This verse is like a light for the ark of salvation,
In the city, he was looking for a beloved and the most intoxicated
[in Allah's love],
As if he was looking for a rebinding request,
May it not be a mirage which would be a threat to his life,
He is the thirstiest of the thirsty, swimming in an ocean of needs!

RESPECT FOR THE SAYYIDS

Narrator: Sayyid Kamal Saadat Shokrabi

We lived in one of the neighbourhoods and my father was one of the old reciters. Mashhadi Hosein, Ibrahim Hadi's father, was one of my father's old friends. The Late Agha Asghar, Ibrahim's brother, was one of my brother's friends and they were always together. This was how I got to know this family. One day when Agha Ibrahim had come to our house, he sat down and kissed my father's hand. I was surprised as he was a champion of sport and wrestling. The whole neighbourhood knew him. Agha Ibrahim said, "You are Sayyids and the children of Lady Fatimah (a). Your respect is obligatory." We started to visit each other more frequently and one day, my father said to Ibrahim, "Take this child (i.e. me) to the gym." I went to Haj Hasan's gym with my father that night after Ibrahim encouraged me to. From that day onwards, I became one of the athletes of that spiritual environment.

Allah is my witness that Ibrahim would act so humbly with me that I would feel embarrassed. Whenever I would come in, he would say loudly, "Send a Salawat for the safety of all Sayyids." He wouldn't enter the ring until I entered. The director of the gym would also say loudly, "Send a Salawat for the ancestors of the Sayyids," and then we would start exercising. Ibrahim's *akhlaq* made me feel proud of being a Sayyid. His *akhlaq* had a great effect on me and many of the other athletes. Everyone loved him and they would talk about his champion-like morale. A man by the name of Agha Abbas would work there who was the standard-bearer for the late Tayyib. He would give the athletes towels. He would respect Ibrahim very much. This old gentleman had seen many of the champions of Tehran, but he would say, "Ibrahim is unequalled." In those days, whenever we would go somewhere, Ibrahim wouldn't let me use my own money. "Working for the Sayyids has blessings," he would say.

When the Revolution succeeded and the war began, I wouldn't see him as often. Whenever he would come on leave from the warfront, he would always be working for the movement. One night, I saw Ibrahim in the neighbourhood of the al-Fath Committee. We sat together and started to speak. He was worried about the future of the Revolution and the government! He had interesting views. I felt that he had learnt a lot about social and political issues. Even though I was working for the IRGC at that time, I didn't know as much as Ibrahim regarding political issues. He would analyse the issues and problems of the Revolution very well and was worried that the enemies of the Revolution would rob the people of their revolutionary spirit. He was worried that the Wilayatul Faqih may be left alone and on the other hand, he was disappointed at the *akhlaq* of some revolutionary fanatics. I remember him saying clearly, "The enemy is attempting to change make the people focus on other things and to make them neutral. When that happens, the Revolution will be destroyed from inside out."

In those first few years of the war, we went to the mosque on the eve of the 23rd night of the month of Ramadan for the night vigil. On the way, we saw many of the youth of our neighbourhood playing football. All of them said salaam to Ibrahim and showed him respect. When there was no one around us, he said, "My dear Sayyid, look, can you see how the youth have become so busy? Football on the eve of the 23rd night of Ramadan! These are the capitals of Islam and the Revolution, they shouldn't be playing on Laylatul Qadr.[15] They must know what to do." He then continued ruefully, "Three, four years have passed since the Revolution, but we have remained unable to explain this to these youths. I am scared a day may come when all that will remain of the Revolution and Islam is the name." He then said, "May Allah give us a good end."

A while after, Ibrahim's recovered from his wounds and he was returning to the warfront. His face had become very luminous. I said, "Agha Ibrahim, if you are martyred, hope never to God, we will all become orphans." He replied, smiling, "What are you talking about? Put your hope in Allah, we are all transient beings." He then said, "You are the son of Lady Fatimah (a), you have a great position in Allah's eyes. Ask Allah to help Imam Khomeini and the Revolution by the right of your mother. You should work for this Revolution to the best of your capability." At the beginning of the

---

15   Laylatul Qadr or the Night of Decree is said to be the night on which the entire fate of mankind is decreed by Allah. It is also the night on which the Holy Quran was revealed upon the Holy Prophet (s). It is either on the 19th, 21st or 23rd eve of Ramadan.

year, we were informed of Ibrahim's martyrdom. Not only me, but all the youth were orphaned. The year after, the light of our gym also shut down. I heard Haj Hasan say, "This place isn't pleasant without Ibrahim."

THE RED BANDANAS

Narrator: Mortaza Parsaeiyan

I met Ibrahim for the first time during the days leading up to the Revolution at Shah Abd al-Azim's shrine. One Thursday night, he said salaam to me as I was parking my motorcycle, asked me how I was then asked, "Which neighbourhood are you from?" I replied, "I live near Khorasan Square. Shaheen Street." He quickly came forward, shook my hand and said, "So we're from the same neighbourhood. We live close to Khorasan Square too." From then on, we would see each other often and that's how we made friends. In the summer of 1979, I went to Kurdistan with one of my friends and we joined Asghar Vesali's troops in the city of Paveh. I was the youngest soldier of the group and Asghar only accepted me because he knew me from our neighbourhood. He had heard that even though I was no older than sixteen, I had been a political prisoner during the Shah's regime and for this reason, he let me join his guerrilla company. Asghar Vesali was a political prisoner before the Revolution and I had even heard that they had ordered his execution, but Allah kept him alive. Asghar came to the west of the country with his wife and was working in Kurdistan. When the fighting started in Paveh, he threw himself into the battlefield. Paveh was the peak of oppression and heroism for Asghar and the forces in his company.

One night when we were stationed in Paveh, Asghar brought a red cloth and tore it into a few pieces. He dubbed his guerrilla company 'The Red Bandanas'. He would say, "The red colour of this cloth reminds us of the blood of Sayyid ash-Shuhada (a). With these pieces of cloth, we announce our readiness for martyrdom." Asghar's company was at most sixty men strong. From this number, more than fifty were martyred during those few years and less than ten of Asghar Vesali's troops are still living. The fighting in Paveh reached an end when Imam Khomeini (ra) delivered his message and many people arose to passionately protect their country. Our next mission was in the town of Mahabad. When I was in the IRGC base in Mahabad, I was surprised to see Ibrahim Hadi. I heard he was working as a teacher, but he had come to Kurdistan after the message of Imam Khomeini (ra). I went forward, said salaam, and asked him how he was. At that moment, Asghar came. I didn't know he knew Ibrahim. Asghar hugged Ibrahim like two old friends. He then asked Ibrahim to join 'The Red Bandanas'. Ibrahim agreed and we left the base with Asghar's forces. People were saying that a group of secession-seeking Kurds had caused a disturbance, but this was far from the truth. We found that many people who were partisans of the royal Pahlavi family were fighting against us, and not one of them was Kurdish. They had seized the opportunity to fight against the Islamic Republic.

Fighting and carrying out guerrilla operations within the city was very difficult and even remembering those days upsets me. For example, there were times when we were besieged inside a house and they were shooting towards us from all directions. My body was trembling from fear, but our spirits would be raised when we would see the bravery of people like Asghar, Ibrahim and the other unknown commanders of 'The Red Bandanas'. Ibrahim was part of 'The Red Bandanas' until the provinces of Kurdistan became relatively safe, but after a short while, the imposed war began. On the first day of the war, Ibrahim was in Tehran. As soon as he heard the news, he went to Kermanshah and from there to Sarpol-e Zahab. I was in the base of 'The Red Bandanas' in Mahabad and I went with them to Sarpol-e Zahab and reached the Abu Zar Base. On the 24th of September 1980, I reached Sarpol-e Zahab. The commanders told us the city of Qasr-e Shirin had been occupied and the enemy would reach Sarpol-e Zahab with a few armoured and infantry brigades within a few hours. The enemy had waged a full-blown war against our Islamic government, and no one knew what was about to happen.

THE ADHAN

Narrator: Mortaza Parsaeiyan

When 'The Red Bandanas' entered Sarpol-e Zahab, we were met by Ibrahim's handsome and luminous face. Asghar Vesali went forward, hugged Ibrahim and asked, "What's up? When did you get here?" Ibrahim replied, "I came here with a few friends from Tehran," and then he spoke about the city. Asghar was made the commander of the very few soldiers in the city. As well as 'The Red Bandanas', Asghar had brought around fifty Kurdish Peshmerga soldiers with himself. While we were organising the troops, we heard reports that an armoured brigade and several infantry battalions of the Iraqi military would reach Sarpol-e Zahab within a few hours. If Sarpol-e Zahab was occupied, it meant both the Abu Zar Base and Kermanshah would be occupied. Therefore, protecting this region was vital. Asghar stationed soldiers in the sensitive areas of the region immediately and with the experience he had gained from Kurdistan, he let the enemy tanks come very close to the city. At Asghar's orders, we caught them unawares and attacked them with our few weapons and ammunition. I will never forget Ibrahim was stationed in one of the trenches and was constantly firing at the enemy with a grenade launcher. The Iraqi military was forced to retreat from Sarpol-e Zahab due to the heroic fighting of our soldiers, but their artillery guns were constantly bombarding the city and our positions. Ibrahim was trying to raise the soldiers' morale as they were terrified.

At noon, Ibrahim said to me, "I'm going on the roof." He stood on the roof of one of the houses at the entrance of the city which wasn't too far away from the enemy. He then picked up a speakerphone and started to recite the adhan! Ibrahim's loud voice reverberated through the region. Ibrahim's adhan mostly influenced our troops. When they heard this heavenly voice, they gained strength of heart. Of course, Ibrahim would recite the adhan always and everywhere. Whenever he would recite the adhan, Asghar Vesali would say, "Well done, well done! This is the best way to increase our morale!" That day when Ibrahim recited the adhan, the enemy started to bombard the city with their artillery guns more than before. Some were saying, "Ibrahim, now is not the time for these things," but he completed his adhan valorously. I remember Ibrahim did the same thing when we were besieged by the anti-revolutionaries in Kurdistan. We were being shot at from all directions and I was trembling like a leaf as I was young. Ibrahim climbed the wall onto the roof, picked up a speakerphone and recited the adhan loudly. You can't imagine how comforting this adhan was for our soldiers. Even the anti-revolutionaries were shaken by the adhan! They thought we were in a position of weakness and on the verge of surrender, but they stopped shooting because of this beautiful adhan recited towards them. However, on that day in Sarpol-e Zahab, the enemy was attacking us from all directions.

The mountains overlooking the city had fallen to the

enemies and they were bombarding the city accurately using the high ground. Under such circumstances, Ibrahim would climb up high three times a day and recite the adhan. Whenever Ibrahim would recite the adhan with his heavenly voice, the enemy would increase their fire. I don't know what they were worried about! I remember one day when I was sitting with Asghar Vesali, Ibrahim and a few others, someone objected to Ibrahim, asking, "Why is it that whenever we are under siege, you recite the adhan, especially with a loud voice and right in the face of the enemy?" Many of the soldiers had the same question, but perhaps they were too afraid to ask. Everyone was waiting for his answer. Ibrahim thought a little and didn't say more than a few sentences from which everyone withdrew their own answer. Ibrahim replied, "Wasn't Imam Husayn (a) besieged in Karbala? Why did they recite the adhan and pray in the face of the enemy?" He then paused and continued, "This is why we fight the enemy with prayer and adhan."

THOSE FOUR PEOPLE

Narrator: Mortaza Parsaeiyan

Many of the soldiers believe that our war transformed into a Holy Defence after the impeachment of Bani Sadr, as in, they believe that the doors of spirituality were opened on us and the soldiers started to pay attention to religious issues. However, I believe that we experienced the Holy Defence from Ibrahim's essence on the warfront of Sarpol-e Zahab at the start of the war. Ibrahim would recite at any opportunity he could find, he would discuss religious issues with the soldiers etc. In those first few days, the commanders would meet in one of the houses of Sarpol-e Zahab where 'The Red Bandanas' were stationed. Asghar Vesali, Ali Teymouri (Asghar's second-in-command), Ibrahim Hadi and General Sheeroudi would attend these meetings. At the end of the meeting, Ibrahim would recite, and all the soldiers would gather to benefit from Ibrahim's angelic voice. One day, I went to the Abu Zar Base on Asghar's behalf to give a letter to General Sheeroudi, telling him to come to Sarpol-e Zahab for a meeting. Agha Sheeroudi said, "Tell him that our friend Agha Ibrahim must be there," and I replied, "Sure, he will also there."

Days passed and Ibrahim's spirituality had a wonderful effect on the soldiers. We would witness the peak of Ibrahim's spirituality when we faced the enemy. He would act with the captive enemy soldiers in a way that he became a role model for all soldiers. I remember during the first few days, we took four soldiers captive on the Kourehmoush Mountains. We were stationed in a house at the entrance of the city. We brought these four captives to the house with Ibrahim so that they could be transferred to the Abu Zar Base within the next few days. On the other side of the courtyard, there was a room with an iron door. Our friends suggested to put the captives in the room and lock the door, but Ibrahim didn't agree. He said, "They are our guests." I replied, "Agha Ibrahim, what are you talking about? These are prisoners of war. They will escape." Ibrahim said, "No, if our *akhlaq* is good, I assure you they won't do anything." He untied the captives' hands and brought them into the room. We laid the table for lunch and I brought the bread and canned food. There wasn't much canned food. According to Ibrahim's rationing, two of us would eat one can of food, but he gave each Iraqi prisoner one can of food! The Iraqis witnessed this themselves; they saw that they were meant to be in chains and shackles, but they were now being treated better than us. They saw we would give the captives better food than ourselves. Two days later, Ibrahim told me to prepare the shower. I turned the boiler on, and the shower was ready. Ibrahim prepared four pairs of underwear and sent each of the Iraqi prisoners to the shower to clean themselves. That afternoon, Ibrahim went to the Abu Zar Base. While he was gone, a vehicle came to pick up the captives from our base. The captives were crying and weren't going! They were constantly calling out for Ibrahim. I called through the radio and Ibrahim returned. The Iraqi captives kissed his hands and face one by one and said farewell to him. They were begging to stay with Ibrahim, but the rules don't allow such a thing. They got into the vehicle and they left. For a few minutes, their eyes remained on Ibrahim. It was as if they didn't want to ever leave. Ibrahim would do these things sincerely and never with the intention of showing off. His inner and outer intentions were the same. I have no doubt that during those three days, Ibrahim changed their view of the Islamic Republic with his sincere actions. I don't know where those captives are right now, but I am sure that they no longer bear animosity towards us.

I have known many martyrs, but I have seen very few with a personality like Ibrahim's. Some shared Ibrahim's traits, but I have never seen someone with as complete a personality as Ibrahim. Ibrahim loved everybody, from the Iraqi captives to the soldiers who had come from every corner of Iran. This love wasn't fake. Ibrahim would help others lovingly. He would get upset if he saw someone was being bothered. Ibrahim never accepted position or commandership. Perhaps one of the reasons behind this was that he may make a wrong decision and place those around him in hardship. For this reason, he would always say, "Let one of the others accept this responsibility and I will help him to the best of my ability."

Ibrahim was very kind and loving towards animals. He couldn't even bear to see an animal suffer. One day, we were meant to go from Gilan-e Gharb to Kermanshah and from there to Tehran. We got on a minibus and set off for Kermanshah. As soon as the bus left the city, it braked suddenly and we heard a sound as if something had hit the bus. The driver stopped for a moment and then continued driving. Ibrahim looked out the window and realised we had stopped because the bus had hit a dog. I could see that the dog's leg was injured and was limping across the road. Ibrahim said to the driver, "Stop, let me see what happened." The driver said, "It's nothing, it was a dog." Ibrahim said louder, "Stop, I want to get off!" The bus stopped. Ibrahim paid two people's fares and we got off. We found the dog, but the poor thing couldn't walk nor bark. Ibrahim approached the dog and examined its leg. He took a piece of wood and made a makeshift brace for the dog's leg with a piece of plastic lying on the side of the road. Even that dog wasn't deprived of Ibrahim's love. One of the native Kurds was watching this from afar. He came closer and was marvelling at Ibrahim's actions. He was happy and started thanking Ibrahim for doing this. Ibrahim gave some money to that person and said, "Look after this one. If you can, bring him some bones." An hour later, Ibrahim and I got on the next minibus. On the way, I was thinking about Ibrahim's actions. He had a wonderful personality. He delayed his journey and put himself into hardship for a dog. Later, I heard a saying from the Holy Prophet (s) which said, "A woman's sins will be forgiven because she was kind to a dog and gave it water."

WILAYAH

Narrator: Mortaza Parsaeiyan

It was October 1980 and the first night of Muharram. They sent a radio message from the Abu Zar Base, asking Brother Hadi to come to the gathering at the base. I knew that Amir Monjar, one of Ibrahim's friends, had some kind of position at the Abu Zar Base. I assumed that they had set up a gathering for the beginning of the month of Muharram. I let Ibrahim know. He took one of the vehicles from Sarpol-e Zahab, came to the base of 'The Red Bandanas' and called me. I came out and Ibrahim said to me, "Get in, let's go to the Abu Zar Base together." I replied, "Asghar Vesali isn't here. He might be upset that I went..." He said, "You have nothing to do here. I will tell the others you came with me." He then told one of our friends, took permission and we left. It was a very nice and simple majlis. Ibrahim was reciting and the soldiers in the base were beating their chests. General Sheeroudi and some of the air force pilots stationed at the base as well as the baseejis, revolutionary guards and soldiers had all gathered and were crying upon the oppression of the Master of Martyrs. The majlis ended at midnight. There was a wonderful spiritual atmosphere.

That night, we were exhausted, so we made arrangements to sleep there. One of the soldiers from the communications department entered the prayer hall and announced, "Brother Hadi, Agha Vesali has sent a message that you must return to Sarpol tonight." While Ibrahim was thinking, I said, "Agha Ibrahim, forget it. It's dark and the rain is pouring down. Let's just go in the morning." Ibrahim stood up and said, "Get up, let's go. Asghar Vesali has Wilayah[16] over us. He is the commander and his order must be executed." I didn't expect Ibrahim to say something like this; he was very friendly with Asghar. He taught me, someone six years younger than him, a lesson. These words lingered in my mind; the order of the commander is the order of Wilayah and executing this order is obligatory. He got ready to leave. I said, "Agha Ibrahim, I have never seen rain as severe as this. We can't drive without headlights in this rain." In those days, the enemy had the area under surveillance and if a car was moving with its

---

16 Meaning guardianship

headlights on, it would be destroyed by the enemy's artillery guns. However, Ibrahim was determined to return. Another problem we had was the car's windscreen wipers didn't work properly. Ibrahim thought a little then said, "Mortaza, sit behind the wheel. I will take off my shirt and I will run in the middle of the road in front of the car in my white undershirt. Follow the white shirt and drive right behind me so that you don't drive off the road." I replied, "What are you talking about, Agha Ibrahim? I don't know how to drive very well. I will run and you drive." I said this and quickly took off my military uniform. Ibrahim shouted, "I won't let you; you have to sit behind the wheel!" but I quickly ran outside and used the excuse that I didn't know how to drive the Simorgh brand of cars. It was raining heavily, and I started to run. Ibrahim was driving behind me and shouting, "Mortaza, come, get in. Let me go outside."

I ran the whole way. I was completely drenched. When we reached our base, I had no energy left in my body. Two of the soldiers ran to bring me a blanket and I changed my clothes quickly. Asghar Vesali looked at both of our conditions and said, "Agha Ibrahim, you could have returned in the morning." Ibrahim said, "It was the order of the commander. Even if stones were falling from the sky, we would return." Asghar lowered his head out of shame and didn't say anything. For a long time after that night, Ibrahim would lower his head in shame whenever we met and say, "That night, you made me very ashamed. If you knew how to drive, I swear to God, I wouldn't let you go in front of the car."

THE BENEFIT OF THE RELIGION

Narrator: Ibrahim Seifzadeh

I went to the warfront at the start of the war and they immediately dispatched me to the Gilan-e Gharb Province. Our commander there was (Shaheed) Hasan Palash and they dispatched us to the town of Bansiran. We were in that area for a while. It was important for us to keep hold of the mountains of that region and they had to be guarded. After a while, we returned to Gilan-e Gharb to rest and to take a shower. We went to a house near the central mosque. It was the base of the IRGC guerrilla troops. When I entered the base, I saw a youth tying provisions and ammunition to a mule while reciting a poem in praise of Amir al-Mu'mineen (a) to himself. He had a very beautiful voice. He then went to the other side of the courtyard and started to do *Varzesh-e Bastani* on a stone plate. I was watching him carefully. It was clear that he was very skilled in *Varzesh-e Bastani* and he had extraordinary bodily strength. When he finished, I went forward and said salaam. He replied warmly with a smiling face. He welcomed me so warmly as if he had known me for years. He asked my name and I told him my name was Ibrahim. He became very happy and said, "I am also Ibrahim. Is it okay if I call you Dash[17] Ibrahim?" I replied, "It's up to you." I fell in love with his good *akhlaq* just by that first interaction. He asked, "Dash Ibrahim, where are you from?" I replied, "Tehran, near Khorasan Square." He said with surprise, "So we are from the same neighbourhood. We live on Mina Street." He took my hand, took me into the building and introduced me to his friends. They all welcomed me very warmly. Ibrahim asked me if I wanted to play table tennis with him. His friends were watching us play. At the start, it was clear he was very skilled at the game and I couldn't return his serves, but gradually, he played in such a way that I was

---

17 Meaning brother

able to tie the score and at the end, I won! That day was a very good day. Since the day I went to the warfront, I was constantly on intelligence and defensive operations and I hadn't made any friends until that day. I was glad that I had made friends with one of the best soldiers on the warfront.

At noon, Ibrahim came into the courtyard and started reciting the adhan. He then gathered everyone for congregational prayers and after prayers, he recited Dua Faraj very beautifully. After prayers, I asked him about the luggage he loaded on the mule. He said, "I'm going on an intelligence operation with some others. I loaded some bread, dates, canned food and ammunition on the mule." After showering, I said farewell to Ibrahim and went back to Bansiran.

A few days later, I came to Gilan-e Gharb on leave to go to Kermanshah with some of the soldiers and from there to Tehran. I was looking for a bus but I couldn't find one. As soon as I reached the IRGC base, I saw my good friend, Ibrahim. He came forward, welcomed me warmly and asked, "What are you doing here, Dash Ibrahim, what's up?" I replied, "I'm going back on leave." "Are you serious?" he exclaimed, "I am also going to Tehran!" This was great news for me; I had found a brilliant travel companion! We went to Kermanshah in an IRGC vehicle and we bought bus tickets from there. We had an hour to spare, so Ibrahim suggested that we go to the hospital and visit the wounded soldiers. After meeting them, we went to the terminal and left for Tehran. Most of the passengers on the bus were soldiers.

As soon as we left the city, the driver made the music louder. Ibrahim then asked everyone to recite a Salawat a few times and everybody did so. He then became silent. I glanced at Ibrahim and I saw he was incensed. He was constantly praising Allah, clenching his fists and closing his eyes. I was scared. I couldn't understand why he was so upset. I realised that it must have been because of the music. I asked, "Agha Ibrahim, has something happened? I think it's because of the music. If you want, I can tell the driver-" He didn't let me finish my words and said, "May I be your sacrifice, go and ask him to turn it off." I went and said to the driver, "Please turn it off if you can." The driver replied, "I can't. I'll fall asleep, I've made a habit of it so I can't." I went back and told Ibrahim what he said. He was looking for a way so that he wouldn't have to listen to the female singer. He had an idea. He pulled a small Qur'an out of his pocket and started to recite the Qur'an beautifully. His voice was so soothing and sweet that everyone started to listen to him. A few minutes later, the driver turned off the music and started to listen to the divine verses. All the passengers were marvelling at his angelic voice. When it was time for Maghrib, he asked me to recite the adhan. Even though my voice was incomparable to his soothing voice, I agreed. I got up and recited the adhan. After that, I never saw Ibrahim again, I learnt great lessons from him during those few days.

THE GUARD

Narrator: Hosein Ghaffari

In January 1981, I set off for the warfront with my classmates from Tehran. We were dispatched to Gilan-e Gharb and remained there for a few months. Allah bestowed upon us the blessing of meeting one of His sincere servants on the warfront. I was a radioman and I had gone on operations several times with Ibrahim. He was like an ordinary baseeji, he would talk and laugh with us but at the same time, he would display his great character. An interesting feature I noticed in Gilan-e Gharb was that there were mules in the base which were familiar with the terrain of the area! The western terrain is uneven, and mules were essential for us. I would see Ibrahim load his ammunition and provisions on a mule and leave. Whenever they would hear the whistling of a mortar shell, these mules would bolt so that they wouldn't be hurt by the debris! However, several stories have been engrained in my memory.

For example, one night, I set off with the intelligence units towards the enemy as a radioman. Ibrahim and one of his friends were pushing a Jeep which had an M40 rifle loaded on it while it was off and placed it in a safe area opposite the enemy. They had designated this area previously. It was directly opposite the enemy's trenches. An hour later, they targeted each enemy trench which had previously been identified and they demolished them. After this, they switched the Jeep on, and we came back quickly before the sun had even risen!

Another story I remember is that in one of the regions, we didn't have a great view of the enemy's positions. Ibrahim put a different plan in action. At night, he would go to the vehicle and hide inside it. I would stay back in our own positions with a radio and I would stay in contact with Ibrahim from a distance. As the sun rose, he would look with binoculars and inform us via the radio. In turn, I would inform the artillery base and they would strike the enemy trenches. The enemy was dumbfounded at how their trenches and positions were under fire one after the other and being demolished so accurately! For this reason, they started to fire missiles blindly. In the afternoon, a mortar shell landed beside the burnt-out vehicle that Ibrahim was hiding in and exploded. Ibrahim's radio suddenly cut off. I was very worried, and I became even more concerned when the sun set. Lest he had been...! Suddenly, I noticed Ibrahim walking towards us slowly. He had been struck by a few small and large pieces of debris. I was so happy. We quickly took him to the hospital. That day, the enemy incurred severe losses.

I was in Gilan-e Gharb until the summer of 1982. After that,

I went to the south and joined the Kumayl Battalion. I was with my battalion on the night before Operation Before the Dawn, but I didn't know that Ibrahim had joined our battalion as part of the intelligence units. I was part of the third company, and we advanced until the third trench under the cover of night. The situation was completely out of our control. The operation failed due to the betrayal of the hypocrites. The soldiers were stuck in the trench and advancing was impossible. A few other soldiers and I went forward a little bit to find a way out but unfortunately, we were besieged and taken captive by the enemy.

During our days in captivity, we would speak with our friends from the Kumayl Battalion who were taken captive after us. They were constantly talking about Ibrahim Hadi's valour in the Kumayl Trench. I was surprised that he had come with our battalion, but I hadn't been able to meet him. Years later, other operations took place and a few of our other friends were also taken captive. During our nights of captivity, they started talking about Ibrahim again. When one of the captives who had just come to the prisoner camp found out that a few others and I knew Ibrahim, he told us about the final days of the operation, the trench, the besiegement and that Ibrahim had been lost at war. When we heard this, the wounds of our hearts were opened once again.

ALLURE

Narrator: Mohammad Khorsheedi

At the start of the war, I was working with the revolutionary committee of the Mohammadi Mosque near the Shaheed Mohallati Highway. My house was behind the mosque in one of the backstreets. A new family moved into our neighbourhood and a few days later, a youth with a very long beard wearing a military uniform went into the house. At first, I thought he was Baluchi as he had an extremely long beard. For this reason, I wasn't happy that they were living opposite from us. I didn't know that he was one of the commanders on the warfront. The next day, he said salaam to me as soon as he left his house and I replied to him, but I was a bit shy as he was older than me.

At night, I would gather at the end of the street and chat with some of my friends. Whenever this youth would pass by, he would smile and say salaam to us. I didn't know who he was nor did I know anything about him. All I knew was he was involved in the war. "A youth has come to our neighbourhood," I said to the head of the committee at the Mohammadi Mosque, "I think he is Baluchi because he has a long beard. I want to make friends with him and bring him to the mosque. He's a good person." He replied, "Okay, bring him." The next day when he said salaam to us, he decided to join us. He spoke a little bit and laughed. I said, "We are going to the Mohammadi Mosque to pray. Will you come with us?" He said yes and we went to the mosque. I was glad that I had managed to bring someone to the committee and the mosque. On the way, some of the youths from the neighbourhood were looking at us strangely. I noticed some were even making fun of my new friend because of his style and appearance. When we entered the mosque, I had thought I had finally encouraged someone to come to the mosque, but suddenly, I saw everyone coming forward. They all greeted him and were asking him about the news from the warfront. When the head of the revolutionary committee saw him, he came forward and said, "Welcome, Agha Ibrahim!" I was lost for words; apparently, I was the only one who didn't know him properly!

From that day onwards, Ibrahim Hadi started attending the Mohammadi Mosque and our friendship grew stronger. All the members of the mosque's revolutionary committee younger than him. Ibrahim had a kind of superiority over them. He would try to do as much as he could to help the people of the mosque.

On Thursday nights, he would spend time with the religious youth until morning and he would then encourage them to pray Fajr in congregation. When prayers ended, he would come to the committee members with a pot full of Haleem.[18] He didn't own anything for himself, neither a motorcycle nor a car, but he would give everything in his possession away sincerely and would spend it on others. Ibrahim's friend owned a Volkswagen. He would bring the car to the mosque on Thursday nights, take some of the youth and go to either the shrine of Shah Abd al-Azim or Behesht-e Zahra. Slowly, Ibrahim became well-known amongst the youth of our neighbourhood. The same youths who were standing at the end of the street and mocked Ibrahim's long beard on the first day were one by one attracted to Ibrahim. He had a great allure. He would always be first to say salaam with a smile. He would never behave rudely, even with the misguided people, and would always attract people to himself one way or another. Most of the youths who would loiter at the end of the road were attracted to him through sport. In the gym, we found out that Ibrahim was a champion of wrestling. He would never talk about himself and that added to the allure of his personality. It reached such a stage that about twenty of us would gather at night and Ibrahim would speak to us. As long as he was with us, he would gather our group and would speak to us. When he was absent, we would talk about him.

Ibrahim was wounded during Operation Fath ol-Mobin and had returned to Tehran for a few months so that his foot could heal. During that period of convalescence, he guided many of the youth of our neighbourhood indirectly in such a manner that when he was returning to the warfront three months later, he took some of those very people who had nothing to do with the Revolution and Islam with him! Many of those people that he trained became commanders of battalions and heads of intelligence.

---

18   A kind of soup made with lentils, pulses and meat and eaten with sugar and cinnamon for breakfast

Years have passed since my short friendship with Ibrahim. The more I ponder over that time, the stronger my belief is that he was perfect role model for practical *akhlaq*. Everything he would do was a lesson for us. We studied a complete course of Islamic *akhlaq* just by watching his *akhlaq*. If someone is searching for a suitable role model to climb the stages of spirituality, he should watch Ibrahim's behaviour and *akhlaq*.

Let me give two examples to prove my point:

There was an imam at one of the mosques in our neighbourhood who was very spiritual but was opposed to the Revolution. This believing old man had nothing to do with the Revolution and he only cared about his prayers. For this reason, the anti-revolutionary forces of our neighbourhood would meet in his mosque. It reached an extent that if someone went to that mosque, the people would say, "So-and-so is affiliating with the anti-revolutionaries." I noticed that when Ibrahim came on leave, he would go to that mosque for a while, especially for Fajr. He had made friends with the imam of the congregation and they would always talk with each other. When I mentioned this in the Mohammadi Mosque, some of the youth of the committee exclaimed, "Ibrahim has gone to the anti-revolutionary mosque!?" A while after Ibrahim's visits to that mosque, we were informed that the imam of that very mosque had requested for a committee[19] to be established in his mosque. A few days later, the imam of the mosque visited the families of a few martyrs and he gradually became one of the most revolutionary scholars in our neighbourhood. Ibrahim didn't say anything, but I had no doubt that this was the fruit of his sincere efforts. That mosque's committee became very active and powerful and it gave thirty martyrs in the way of resistance during the war. Also, the imam of this congregation was the real supporter of the revolutionaries of this mosque.

Another example of Ibrahim's Islamic *akhlaq* was how he

---

19 Every revolutionary mosque in Iran has a revolutionary committee so when the word committee comes, we are referring to such committees

made friends with one of the people from our neighbourhood. There was a household in our neighbourhood which strongly opposed the Revolution and loved the Shah. The father of the family owned a truck covered in photos of the Shah and the royal crown. The sons were worse than the father. They were all hooligans and involved in knife fights. One of his sons was even more eager to do evil acts. He served his compulsory military service and was discharged when Khorramshahr[20] was liberated. He would mock the religious youth more than the others. He would always try to harass people and he loved hooliganism. Those who lived during that time will understand what I am talking about better. I couldn't understand how Ibrahim could change such a person! One time, the youth came to the end of the road and asked us, "Guys, have you seen my friend, Agha Ibrahim?" I exclaimed, "Your friend!?" He replied, "We were meant to go and exercise together. I was waiting for him, but he's late." I thought to myself, "He is known as the hooligan of Mina Street, but he has fallen in love with Ibrahim! If Ibrahim stays for another year and doesn't return to the warfront, there will no longer be any kind of evil in our neighbourhood."

This same person started going to the mosque with Ibrahim a short while later. At first, he didn't know how to pray, but he learnt over time. A while later, I saw him on the warfront. Ibrahim wouldn't take everyone with him to the Intelligence Department, but he took him to the Intelligence Department and would use his special morale to his advantage. Eventually, the Intelligence Department considered him the bravest soldier of their department. Years after Ibrahim's martyrdom, I met one of my friends from the Operation Preparation Department. I asked about the person, but I didn't tell him anything about his past. My friend asked, "Are you talking about Haj So-and-so? He is one of the pillars of the Intelligence Department. When you go on an intelligence

---

20 A city on the border between Iraq and Iran, an area where many Iranian soldiers were martyred trying to liberate the city, hence, earning the nickname 'The City of Blood'

operation with him, you feel relaxed as he is very skilled at his job and he is a very believing person."[21] I thought to myself, "Well done to Ibrahim! He trained such people out of hooligans in our neighbourhood."

JAHANSHAH

Narrator: Ali Sadeghi

Life on the warfront was very difficult, especially in conditions where we were forced to stay away from our cities for several consecutive weeks. Some of my friends couldn't tolerate being in such an environment for so long. I remember clearly that some of the soldiers would become depressed and suffer from mental illnesses after staying in the region for a while. The cure for their problem to ensure that they wouldn't suffer from mental illness was social activities. Games, jokes, and laughter would resolve these people's problems. Ibrahim was an expert in this field. Ibrahim's and his friends' jokes would always make everyone smile. When we were bored, he would start playing a game everyone could join in with. One time, our friends from the IRGC came to Gilan-e Gharb from the south. Ibrahim was sitting with them with some of his friends and we could only hear them laughing. I joined them and asked Ibrahim, "What are you doing?" He joked, "Do you want us to cry?" He then very casually started to cry, and tears rolled down from his eyes. Another time, we were sitting with the soldiers from the Andarzgu Battalion and the imam of Friday prayers of one of the

---

21   This great person is now a veteran and one of the living martyrs of the era of Holy Defence

central cities of Iran had come to visit the soldiers. The scholar removed his libas[22] to perform ritual ablution so that he could pray. Ibrahim quickly took permission and put on the scholar's libas. He then went to show the others.

Ibrahim had a friend from Kermanshah who was better friends with him than the others. Their friendship was very interesting in its own right. He was a youth two metres tall with a large and powerful physique. The first time I met him was when I went to Kermanshah with Ibrahim to meet Haj Agha Eslami. Ibrahim introduced him to me, saying, "This is Agha Jahanshah, one of my friends." When I shook Jahanshah's hand, Ibrahim signalled to squeeze my hand a little. Believe me, whenever I think of that moment right now, all the bones in my hand start to hurt. When Jahanshah shook my hand, he put some pressure on my fingers. I screamed and when I pulled my hand away, my fingers stuck to one other! That night, I stayed with Ibrahim, Jahanshah and Agha Eslami. For dinner, they brought seven chickens with bread. We all ate one chicken between us and Jahanshah ate six chickens with bread alone! After we ate dinner, he picked up a jar of jam and started to eat it plain with a spoon. "What is this friend of yours doing," I signalled to Ibrahim, "How much does he eat?" Ibrahim whispered very quietly, "Tonight, he wants to sleep peacefully and so, he ate less than normal!" After dinner, they brought a plank to do traditional push-ups and Jahanshah started to exercise. One of our friends sat on Jahanshah's back, but it was as if he hadn't eaten that much for dinner. We went back the day after.

A while later, we went to Kermanshah with Ibrahim. We had received reports that a few locals had started arguing with two soldiers, and a fight was close to breaking out. One of the locals informed us, "They have gone to bring one of their strongest friends so that they can start a fight." I became a bit worried; if a fight broke out, it would be very hard to deescalate the situation.

---

22   The ceremonial robes of a scholar consisting of a turban (imamah) and cloak (aba)

We went to the area with Ibrahim. An hour later, we saw a few of the locals coming towards the base with a man who looked like a gangster. When they came closer, Ibrahim went towards them and shouted at the top of his voice, "Jahanshah, how are you?!" Jahanshah, who was much taller than everyone, came forward and started to greet all of us. The locals were looking at us in awe. Ibrahim showed courtesy to the locals and greeted each of them warmly. In conclusion, this friendship turned a fight into peace and friendship.

That year, Jahanshah came to Tehran and was arrested for something he did. In prison, he said to the jailer, "Open these handcuffs, they're hurting me. I'll open them myself otherwise," but the jailer just laughed. Jahanshah pulled his hands apart and broke the handcuffs. He then twisted an old two-toman coin in front of the other prisoners. Believe me, if he had taken part in a contest for the strongest man, no one would be able to beat him. However, a year later, our friends informed us that Jahanshah had died in a car crash. The other soldiers and I couldn't believe it. We joked, "A normal car can't take that man down!" but they replied, "Actually, he crashed into a truck on the road to Hamadan."

SHIYAKOUH

Narrator: Hosein Ghazanfari

In 1981, I was serving as a commando in the Armed Forces. I had the responsibility of organising the ammunition for the 58th Dhul-Fiqar Brigade. The Dhul-Fiqar Commando Brigade was one of the exemplary and active brigades of the military and gave many martyrs. The soldiers of this brigade had a revolutionary spirit and would take part in most operations alongside the IRGC and the baseejis. To prove the revolutionary morale of this brigade, it is enough to say that when they were looking for soldiers to send to

Syria and Lebanon, three battalions were sent from the Mohammad Rasulullah (s) Division and three were to be sent from the Armed Forces, all of them from the 58th Dhul-Fiqar Commando Brigade.

There were several factors as to why the commanders and soldiers of this brigade were so courageous, especially towards the beginning of the war, and perhaps one of these factors was because they had a warrior by the name of Ibrahim Hadi fighting alongside them. In 1981, I was constantly travelling between the cities of Gilan-e Gharb and Islamabad and other various cities because of my responsibilities. The Dhul-Fiqar Brigade was stationed in Gilan-e Gharb. I have noted my memories of those days down and for that reason, I can accurately narrate my stories. On exactly the 23rd of September 1981, I found that a relatively large crowd had gathered in a place known as Cheshmeh-ye Sarab as I was leaving the city of Gilan-e Gharb. I got off and went towards the crowd. Cheshmeh-ye Sarab was where the soldiers would go swimming and take a bath. When I went closer, I noticed that some people were doing *Varzesh-e Bastani* and the others were watching them. There was a handsome youth busy playing the drums next to the ring whilst reciting beautiful poems loudly. The people had gathered and were enjoying watching them exercise. I asked one of my friends, "Who is this youth? He has such a beautiful voice." He exclaimed, "Don't you recognise him!? This is Ibrahim Hadi, a youth from Tehran and the warrior of the west of the country."

I still remember my first meeting with Ibrahim after all these years. After that, I wished to see him once again. A few days later, I went to the IRGC base in Gilan-e Gharb to do something and I asked if I could meet Agha Ibrahim Hadi. The IRGC soldiers recognised me and replied, "He has gone to the Bazi-Deraz Mountains with the soldiers of the Andarzgu Guerrilla Battalion. I think they're on an intelligence operation." I was strangely eager to meet this youth, so I went to Bazi-Deraz. I saw some of our soldiers in a place called Imam Hasan (a) Riverbank. I paused and then continued walking towards them. The first person to greet me from their group was Ibrahim himself with his luminous face. He said salaam, asked me how I was and hugged me as if he had known me for many years. After exchanging pleasantries, I said, "I came here to visit you. If I can do anything, I am at your service."

After that, we met several times in Gilan-e Gharb. He would greet me warmly every time he saw me and make me feel at home. A while later, I was informed that Operation Matla' al-Fajr was underway. From then on, I had no rest as we had to build trenches and take the boxes of ammunition to the operation line. I would go to the warfront and meet my dear friend every day. Operation Matla' al-Fajr began on the 11th of December 1981 and it achieved most of its goals within two days, distancing the enemy from the border cities and liberating many areas of our Islamic country. Shiyakouh and Bazi-Deraz were the only two places we weren't able to finish our work in. Bazi-Deraz itself is a long story. However, Shiyakouh is a mountain range close to Gilan-e Gharb, and the tallest peak overlooked the whole area. Shiyakouh held great importance for Iraq and therefore, the most resistance we faced in Shiyakouh throughout the operation. Some of the best soldiers of the IRGC and commanders like Jamal Tajeek were martyred in this area, but Shiyakouh was still occupied. We had liberated half the mountain range, but the western side of the mountain range was still in the hands of the enemy. After the operation, the third and fourth battalions of the Dhul-Fiqar Brigade were stationed in and around Shiyakouh.

On the 4th of February, two battalions from the military in Shiraz swapped places with the soldiers of the Dhul-Fiqar Brigade. The third and fourth battalions returned at night and got ready to go on leave. That night, the enemy noticed that our forces were swapping so they attacked our line and bombarded us until sunrise. In the morning, a few commanders and the soldiers of those two battalions came back. As I was still in the area, I asked them what had happened and they replied, "Shiyakouh has fallen. All our forces have been destroyed." We went with their commanders to the base of the Dhul-Fiqar Brigade. They explained to Colonel Ali Yari, the commander of the brigade, that they were attacked before they had even reached the trenches. I left the commander's tent. I was thinking about how much blood had been spilt to liberate Shiyakouh and now we had lost it so easily. I remember well that Major Jafari, the commander of the fourth battalion, was extremely upset and was saying, "If only we didn't swap!" Major Tokhmechi, the commander of the third battalion, was also standing there and didn't know what to do.

Two motorcycles were coming towards us from afar. I became happy and went forward when I saw who was driving the first motorcycle. It was him himself, my good friend Ibrahim! The four people got off the motorcycles and went towards the tent of the commander of the brigade. Ibrahim shook my hand and hugged me with a smile even though he was irate. He then asked if the colonel was there and I said yes. The four people went inside and the three people accompanying Ibrahim started to speak. They explained why it was important to attack Shiyakouh that night and if they didn't do this, the enemy wouldn't allow them to continue the operation in the future by creating more obstacles. The colonel said, "I don't have the power to give such an order. I have to-" Ibrahim interrupted him and said, "Colonel, we will act if you can't." Colonel Ali Yari looked Ibrahim in the eye and said, "No my dear, we are at your side, but allow us to make a correct decision. I will tell you in an hour." Ibrahim and his friends were sitting beneath a tree in perimeter of the brigade's base, waiting for the colonel to tell them. I went and spoke with them for a little bit. I assumed that the people who had come with him were commanders in the IRGC as they knew a lot about the region. Ibrahim introduced them to me. The youth who was sitting on the motorcycle with Ibrahim was Mahmoud Shahbazi, the IRGC commander in Hamadan, the other was Mohsen Vezvaei and the last was Ali Movahhed Danesh.[23] An hour later, I went to the colonel to find out their decision. Colonel Ali Yari asked, "Do you recognise the youth who said we will act ourselves?" Before I could say anything, Major Tokhmechi said, "I know him well, he is known as the hero of Bazi-Deraz." He continued, "Colonel, this youth will hold you and me on his back, take us to the top of Bazi-Deraz and back down again! For as long as I've stayed in Gilan-e Gharb, he has set up sessions of *Varzesh-e Bastani* and I try to participate in this youth's sessions. He has his head screwed on properly." The Colonel agreed with a nod of his head and said, "Delay the soldiers from leaving. We have an operation tonight."

CONQUEROR OF THE PEAK

Narrator: Hosein Ghazanfari

I quickly and gladly gave the order to transfer the ammunition. Three battalions from the Dhul-Fiqar Brigade and three battalions from the IRGC completed the necessary coordination. All the commanders were saying that the whole Shiyakouh Mountain Range must be liberated, including the peak. I have written the details of this event in my diary. At five o'clock in the afternoon on the 5th of February 1982, we started the battle with our artillery guns. As the sun was setting, our troops began to advance. The soldiers from the Armed Forces advanced quite far. On the other side, the soldiers of the IRGC and the baseejis had also advanced. The third and fourth battalions of the Dhul-Fiqar Brigade were moving towards the peak and I heard the commander of the third battalion say with courage over the radio, "I want to be the first person to set foot on the peak of Shiyakouh!" The major was valorously encouraging his troops to advance and an hour later, it was announced on the radio, "The peak of Shiyakouh has

---

23   All three were air force commanders who were to be martyred later on

been liberated!" The third battalion had reached the peak. I was overjoyed. We could hear the soldiers of the IRGC and Armed Forces calling out Allahu Akbar in the region. The enemy had turned on their heels, and we had set up a military hospital in one of the caves at the foot of Shiyakouh. Everyone was excited for this victory which had been achieved by Major Tokhmechi, the commander of the third battalion. He had been shot in the leg, yet he wouldn't let us send him back despite our insistence. He said, "Bandage it, I want to go back to my forces." When we were there, he said something I couldn't understand! While they were bandaging the major, he turned to me and remarked, "I was put to shame by Ibrahim Hadi!"

Anyhow, Shiyakouh was liberated by our heroic soldiers. A few days after, I saw the major whose leg had healed. He called me over and said, "Come here, let me tell you something. Do you remember I had told you I was put to shame by Ibrahim Hadi?" I said yes and he continued, "I am known as the conqueror of Shiyakouh among the soldiers of the of the Dhul-Fiqar Brigade. They even gave me gifts and a medal, all because of something I said over the radio. Everyone is saying I was the first person to conquer the trenches atop the peak, but I must confess something." The major took a deep breath and continued, "That night, the enemy was putting up a strong resistance from their trenches on top of the peak. They didn't want to lose those trenches without a fight. When I approached the peak with our troops, I attacked the trenches on the peak all on my own so I could finish off the remaining troops and become the conqueror of the peak, but to my surprise, there were no enemies there. They had either fled before I arrived or been killed. The floor was littered with corpses. I was glad I had conquered the peak and I announced it over the radio, but suddenly, I saw something unbelievable! Right next to the trenches on the peak, a young soldier was prostrating towards the Qibla and thanking Allah. He then suddenly arose from the dust, facing me.

At first, I was afraid, but then I realised he was Iranian because of his scarf. He had reached the peak before me and had cleared the area himself, but he didn't say anything and fell into prostration and was thanking Allah for this victory. He then got up, hugged me and congratulated me. After that, he went back to his own troops by going down the mountain from the other way without saying anything else." My interest was piqued when he said this. We all thought the major was the conqueror of the peak but now he was saying that someone else had conquered the peak. "Who are you speaking about?" I exclaimed, "Who was this warrior?!" Staring deep into my eyes, the major said, "The conqueror of the peak of Shiyakouh, the hero of Bazi-Deraz, Ibrahim Hadi!"

From then on, whenever the major spoke about Ibrahim, he would call him the hero of Bazi-Deraz. He would say, "No one truly knows this youth!" I remember Colonel Ali Yari also said, "The conquest of Shiyakouh is owed to that youth who said firmly, 'We will act if you can't.'" From that day onwards, my friendship with Ibrahim became stronger. He had become a legend for me and the other soldiers of the Armed Forces. From then on, many of the soldiers of the Armed Forces had an affinity towards him. Despite his heroic achievements, Ibrahim never spoke about himself.

A month later, one of the soldiers called me and said, "A youth has come and wants to see you." I replied, "I don't know anyone here," but I went to the door of the base, nevertheless. To my surprise, Ibrahim was at the door. After exchanging pleasantries, he said, "I came to say goodbye, we're going to the south." I was very upset and said farewell to him. Even though I wasn't from Tehran, I took his address and said, "I would really like to see you again." Operation Fath ol-Mubin began towards the end of March 1982 and for this reason, Ibrahim and his friends went to the south. A few of our battalions also took part in the operation and towards the end, I also went to the south. One night, I was accompanying the commander of the third battalion, Major Tokhmechi. He asked me, "By the way, have you heard from Ibrahim Hadi lately?" and I replied in the negative. The major continued, "I saw him in Ahwaz Airport a few days ago. He was wounded and a piece of shrapnel had struck his chest. They wanted to transfer him to Tehran, but he wanted to return. The doctors bandaged his chest and we returned together."

I saw the major again towards the end of February 1983 who had been promoted to colonel because of his bravery and courage and again, we started to speak about Shiyakouh and Ibrahim Hadi. He asked, "Have you heard from the hero of Bazi-Deraz? Do you know where he is?" As I had heard the story of the Kumayl Trench, I said yes with sorrow. The colonel understood everything from my face and asked again with worry, "Where is Ibrahim?" I told him the story of the siege and the Kumayl Trench in Operation Before the Dawn and I added, "Ibrahim stayed with them and no one has heard from him."

THE EXEMPLARY PERSONALITY

Narrator: Ahmad Ostad-Baqer

The specialists in nurturing say that if you want to nurture a youth correctly and place him on the path you want him to follow, you must first conquer his heart. You must do something for the youth to accept you as a complete role model. They say that youth will accept somebody with at least one of the following characteristics as a role model:

First, you must have a pleasant face and secondly, you must be a sportsman and be able to do things which others aren't. Thirdly, you must have a good voice. Singers or reciters will either willingly or unwillingly become role models for the youth. Most importantly, if you wish to conquer the heart of a youth, you must have good *akhlaq* and pay respect to their opinions. You must be able to joke, laugh and do things by which the youth will enjoy your company. When you put these characteristics from the specialists together, be sure that you will see Ibrahim Hadi's personality. Ibrahim had a heavenly and handsome face and looking at his face would please the people. Regarding Ibrahim's athleticism, I should say nothing, but I remember in one of my first meetings with Ibrahim, he was busy doing push-ups so I started to count how many he did. Eventually, I became tired. His push-ups were just like walking for you and me; no one counts their steps or takes pride in them. He was a professional in every sport, be it volleyball, wrestling, or table tennis. I remember that Ibrahim would shoot with one hand meaning, that he wouldn't put the weapon's sling over his shoulder whilst shooting. He was so strong and experienced that he would shoot like this.

The next topic is his good voice. Ibrahim had such a good voice that many fell in love with it. Sometimes, he would recite poetry in praise of the Ahlulbayt (ams). Also, when he was requested to recite at a majlis, he would perform to his best. In Gilan-e Gharb, we had a Qur'an reciter who knew the rules very well, but Ibrahim had a special passion in his voice when it came to reciting the Qur'an. Everybody loved Ibrahim's recitation of the Qur'an.

When the time for joking and laughter came, he had a good sense of humour and even if we sat with him for more than two hours, we wouldn't feel tired, and this wasn't only felt by me, but rather, all my friends feel the same way. Everyone accepted Ibrahim as a role model. When the commander of the military wanted to do something, he would have to give his reasons and logic behind the decision for people to accompany him, but Ibrahim didn't have to show his reasoning or logic. As soon as he would say that he wanted to do something, we would follow his orders as we had accepted him as our leader.

On the other hand, Ibrahim's personality was worthy of being idolised as he would try to behave according to the commands of the religion. Towards the beginning of the war, there were two kinds of people. The first group were the religious people who were known as the 'Maktabis' and the second group were known as 'Dāsh Moshtīs'. These Dāsh Moshtīs would strongly abide by the law. Honour and chivalry flowed through their veins. Sometimes, some troublemaking or common language would be seen from them, but when it was time to fight, they would fight very courageously. On the contrary to some of my friends, I place Ibrahim in the second group. He was a Dāsh Moshtī. He would indirectly train us with his actions, and he was a complete role model for all the soldiers, and I say with courage that no one was at a loss when they sat with him. If a time arose when there was nothing to do, he would talk, laugh, play with his soldiers and fill their time, and when the time came, he would teach us to be respectful to the higher-ranking officers and the commanders. As well as all these issues, I must remind you that Ibrahim didn't wish to lead. He had been a commander before, but he didn't wish to become a commander or take any responsibility, but he would help the commanders a lot.

He was a good judge of character. He would know information that we would discover after much research. Towards the beginning, small groups had come to spy on the warfront and some simple people had been deceived by them. A few people from these groups came to Gilan-e Gharb, but Ibrahim quickly did research on them and didn't allow us to join them. Another of Ibrahim's well-known characteristics was covering up others' mistakes. If someone made a mistake, he would never say anything to us, and he would also protect his relationship with that person. Later, we would learn that he had personally and privately talked and explained [his mistake] to him. Ibrahim was a confidante to many people, even the commanders. He had a kind heart, and everybody considered him trustworthy.

He wasn't after fame and hated people who would drag others back to reach their own goals. He believed that people should have time to themselves. Despite having a job, he would set a time of privacy, privacy between him and Allah. It was these issues which made Ibrahim a complete role model.

Regarding myself, towards the beginning of the war, I was dispatched to the warfront. I hadn't been through any kind of military training and was young. When I reached the west, they sent me to Gilan-e Gharb and as I stayed in that area, I became familiar with some of the active and well-known soldiers, one of them being Ibrahim. I always thank Allah for placing him on my path of life. He taught me how to live correctly in that short time and taught me lessons which require a long book to be retaught. Later, I became a teacher and I studied many books in the field of nurturing and training, and for this reason, I believe that Ibrahim should be a role model for everybody.

ALLAHU AKBAR

Narrator: Ahmad Ostad-Baqer

Being at Ibrahim's side changed my behaviour and *akhlaq* completely. We held someone who gave no value to the most valuable worldly blessings as a role model. I had seen Ibrahim buy an expensive Shah Maqsood rosary many times. This rosary would truly adorn Ibrahim's hand. When one of his friends said, "You have such a beautiful rosary," Ibrahim gifted it to him immediately. He did this not only with his rosary, but I had also witnessed him giving his shirt away many times! I had a beautiful ring which my mother had bought for me from Mashhad. I took very good care of my ring until one day, one of the soldiers started to stare at my ring and he liked it. I took the ring off at once and gifted it to him. The only thing going through my mind at that moment was Ibrahim's actions. I was sure that if he was here, he would do the same. These were the indirect effects of his actions.

A lesson I learnt from Ibrahim which was very useful for me was the lesson of *'Allahu Akbar'*. This noble praise is repeated during prayers, but not in the way Ibrahim would pay attention to the reality of it. Ibrahim would say, "Do you truly know what *Allahu Akbar* means? It means that Allah is greater than anything you have in mind. Allah is more majestic than anything you can think of, meaning that no one can help you and me more than Him. Allahu Akbar means that this great God is beside us, and who are we?! It is He who helps us in the most difficult circumstances." For this reason, he taught us to shout *'Allahu Akbar'* in every situation, especially when we are stuck. He also showed great heroism in the operations with this same praise of Allah. He would say, "By repeating this praise, your trust in Allah increases."

In 1982, Ibrahim was in Tehran as he was wounded. In Operation Moslem ibn Aqeel, our battalion was meant to infiltrate a place by the name of Miyan-Tang. We were divided into three groups and meant to advance on a previously distinguished path. Our group were travelling along the centre and for some reason, the commanders didn't have hope in our group. They didn't think that we would be able to achieve our goals. Therefore, they told the commanders of our two adjacent groups that when they liberate the area, they should also clear the centre as well. The fight began. We stumbled across a minefield and some were martyred and some wounded. The operation was advancing with great difficulty in our positions and it was no different where the other two groups were positioned. We advanced and two trenches were belonging to the enemy blocking the way on us. In the first trench, there was a soldier with a machine gun and in the second, there was a soldier with an RPG. There was nothing behind these two trenches and we would be able to liberate the area if we cleared the trenches, but they were putting up strong resistance. Our distance from the enemy was less than twenty metres and we were stuck in a few trenches. We didn't have enough courage to even lift our heads. Suddenly, I remembered Ibrahim and his shouts of *'Allahu Akbar'*. I thought to myself that if Ibrahim was here, he would do the same. Our forces were no more than ten or fifteen people, but I cried, "Shout *Allahu Akbar* with belief!" We started to shout as loud as we could and suddenly, we couldn't hear the Iraqis shooting anymore. We carefully lifted our heads and saw that Iraqis had run down the hill and were fleeing. We cleared the trenches and the central positions. With those few troops and the strength of *'Allahu Akbar'*, we cleared the positions to our left so that the group on that side could also advance. We then continued to the positions to our right and by shouting the same slogan, the enemy immediately retreated. The group which had no hope for success managed to liberate the positions of the other groups with a lesson that they had been taught by Ibrahim.

I remember that when we used to go on operations, we would take as many weapons and ammunition as we could, but Ibrahim would take practically nothing. He had a wonderful trust in Allah. When we would ask the reason for this, he would say, "When the battle commences, enough weapons and ammunition will be available for me!" He would then continue, "With the first bullet or missile fired which indicates the start of the battle, some of the soldiers fall to the ground and so, they won't be able to use their weapons or ammunition, and at that time, I use them and in its place, I try to take other tools." He was speaking the truth as I witnessed many times that he would go forward without a weapon and when the battle would commence, he would use the weapons that had fallen to the ground.

BEHIND ENEMY LINES
Narrator: Ahmad Ostad-Baqer

The coordination for Operation Matla' al-Fajr was carried out swiftly and we prepared ourselves for the operation to reduce the pressure of the enemy on Bostan. The plans for an extra operation were drawn up by the military in Gilan-e Gharb. It was arranged that the best troops would go behind the enemy's lines with ammunition and explosives and attack their artillery guns and the commanding base of the enemy's brigades which would coincide with the beginning of the main operation. This would help us to achieve success in the operation and reach our goals on the main lines. Fifteen people including myself were chosen for this operation and the commandership of this group was given to one of Ibrahim's friends by the name of (Shaheed) Ali Khorramdel.

Two days before the operation, we set off with Ibrahim. Ibrahim took us through the valleys on the border and returned. Each of us, as well as wielding a weapon, had a large rucksack full of equipment, ammunition and food. Agha Khorramdel also had a PRC radio to carry out necessary communication. We were ten kilometres away from the warfront and stationed ourselves on a hill close to the Iraqi artillery and their commanding base. We would rest by day and work by night. It was arranged that as the operation started, the artillery would fall because of us on the first stage and then we would attack the commanding base of the enemy which was supposedly their think tank.

Two fearful days passed. In a way, we were sacrificial troops as the chances of us returning were slim, but on the other hand, each one of us was strong and willing to fight. In those two days when we were hiding among the hills and valleys in the enemy's territory, our food was canned fish and aubergine. I remember that I opened a can of aubergine and it was filled with oil. There was no way to heat it either. When I ate the first morsel, it was so spicy, I wasn't able to swallow it. It would have been easier for me to eat plain bread.

The main operation began on the 11th of December 1981. We had gained all the necessary intelligence needed for the operation in the nights before. Agha Khorramdel had given everybody their roles and the plan of attack had been drawn out well. Those were strange moments; we were waiting for the order to attack so that we could finish off the enemy's artillery on the warfront, but nothing was heard from the radio! Agha Khorramdel called them several times, but the commanders told us to not to attack yet. We realised from all the movement and the shooting from the artillery that a severe battle must have taken place in Shiyakouh. Two days passed after the beginning of the operation and we had received no order. They would always tell us to be patient no matter how many times we called. They were held in Shiyakouh and there was no way for them to advance in the main fronts.

On the evening of the second day, they called us very briefly and told us that the commander of the operation has banned us from carrying out any kind of action! All of us were shocked by this news. A few of them said to the commander of the group, "Iraq has closed off all routes for us so we can neither advance nor return. We neither have food and this means..." Another said, "The best thing we can do now is to attack and eventually, we will either be killed or taken captive, but at least we would be able to damage their artillery." I and the others were very anxious and stressed. What were we to do?! Our provisions had nearly finished, and the base was no longer answering our calls. They would merely tell us not to carry out any operation. There was no way back either as the Iraqis had filled the valley we needed to pass through to return to our troops. We were at the peak of hopelessness and it was gradually becoming dark. Our local guide also abandoned us when he heard this news!

We heard a sound from the radio again and a weak voice was calling Ali Khorramdel. Ibrahim Hadi was on the other end and he was calling Ali. We all ran towards the radio and Ibrahim started to speak, "Ali dear, all the routes on the border are full of troops. I have tried several routes for your return, but there is no way except one. Gather the troops and move to the north of where the operation is being carried out. When you walk a few kilometres north, you will reach a tall mountain. The enemy is stationed on the west and east foot of the mountain, but they aren't at the peak. I will come up from this side of the mountain and you come up from the back so that we can go back together."

Two of the people had fallen ill and it had started to rain. We started to advance with hardship, but it was as if the route would never end. We reached the mountain towards midnight and Ibrahim was waiting for us on the other side. He had come for us with a motorcycle and a radio. We started to climb the mountain. It was a very tall mountain and however much we climbed, we didn't reach the mountain. We had only climbed less than halfway up the mountain, but Ibrahim had reached the peak with his strong body. He then came down towards us. You can't imagine how much morale we gained from meeting Ibrahim after a few days of hopelessness. We all hugged him. I looked at him momentarily and noticed that his knee was drenched in blood. I asked him what had happened. He didn't give a proper answer, but I figured that when he came towards us, he had turned the motorcycle's lights off and travelled on the sandy roads. He must have fallen hard onto the ground in this state. When Ibrahim saw the state of the ill people, he organised the group. He gave the healthy people a few rucksacks to bring with themselves and he carried one of the sick and exhausted members of the group on his back despite his wounded leg. He carried him on his back for a few kilometres up the mountain. An hour later, we reached the top of the peak and we set off towards our own troops. We prayed Fajr in that state and reached our own forces before sunrise. On the way, Ibrahim made a call and arranged for a van to transfer us. The sun had risen when we got into the van and set off towards Gilan-e Gharb.

We slept for the next forty-eight hours. Of course, this

was natural, but Ibrahim started to serve in another area after the injury on his leg was bandaged. It was as if this person didn't understand the meaning of exhaustion! Later, I asked my friends at the base what had happened. They said, "On the second night, it was announced that we were to leave those fifteen people alone and that we weren't going to continue the main operation. In that same meeting, Ibrahim asked what the fate of those people would be as they wouldn't be able to return? The commander of the operation replied, "In the best-case scenario, they will be taken captive!' As the lives of the soldiers were very important to Ibrahim, he started to shout and swear, saying things like if your brother or son was with them, would you say the same?!" He then contacted Haj Hosein Allah-Karam and said, "I'm going to find a way for those people to return." Haj Hosein gave a radio to him and said, "Do whatever you can.""' In conclusion, fourteen others and I, or in better terms, fifteen families owe the return of their youth to Ibrahim's struggles and sacrifice that night. He didn't sleep on the first night of the operation either, but he bore the fatigue to save us. A few days later and in the continuation of Operation Matla' al-Fajr, the story of 'The Pomegranate Hills' and the miracle of the adhan took place.

INSIGHT

Narrator: Commander Amir Nowhi

My friends and I were the fifteen people who were chosen to destroy the enemy's artillery and were besieged behind the enemy's lines in the first stage of Operation Matla' al-Fajr. We had gone to destroy the enemy's artillery, but the operation didn't go to plan. It was there that Ibrahim came to our rescue. That was the first time I got to meet him, but I was severely wounded in the next stage of the operation and my hand was paralysed. I had no choice but to go to a clinic in Tehran even though I was from Kermanshah.

When Ibrahim heard about this, he didn't let me stay anywhere else. He took a few days of leave and came with me. I was a guest at Ibrahim's house for a few days and I was a great burden on his family, especially his mother. He borrowed a motorcycle from one of his friends and was always helping with my medical work. After that, I said to my friends that there is a youth in Tehran who is better at serving guests than the Kurds.[24]

I must say that when I was with Ibrahim in Tehran, I witnessed that most of the people of his neighbourhood were friends with him. When Ibrahim would come out, he would say salaam to everyone. Many young children made friends with him because he would greet them all the time. Many ordinary people who I wouldn't greet were friends with Ibrahim. I remember that one day, we came out of the street together and a few scholars with a neat and beautiful appearance were coming towards us. From what I knew of Ibrahim, I thought to myself, "He will say salaam and talk with them for a little bit," but contrary to my expectations, he didn't even say salaam to them! I looked at him with surprise. He understood what was going through my mind and for this reason, he said, "These scholars are Wilaei. I have nothing to do with this group!" I asked what Wilaei meant and he said, "It refers to people who don't accept anything other than the Wilayah of the Ahlulbayt (ams); not the Wilayat ul-Faqih nor going to the warfront. They only value the Wilayah of Ali (a). I have spoken to them several times, but it to no avail as they only accept their own beliefs." He then continued, "They are a great danger to the Revolution and Islam. They are like the Khawarij[25] who were involved in Imam Ali (a)'s government." That day, I couldn't understand what Ibrahim was saying as his level of understanding was greater than the rest of us, but years later, I understood what insight Ibrahim had with the establishment of the Shirazi faction and the English Shias.

---

24   The Kurds are famed for their good etiquette with guests.

25   They were a group of people who revolted against Imam Ali (a) and believed that no one had the right to rule except Allah himself

I am from Kermanshah and grew up in a large religious family. Towards the beginning of my youth, I met Ibrahim in Gilan-e Gharb, but Allah knows how much influence he had on my life. I still haven't met a person as effective as him till now even though many years have passed since then. I studied a complete course of beliefs and *akhlaq* just by being his companion. Let me give an example. He familiarised us with the sport of champions and during exercise, he would praise Allah and recite supplication, therefore teaching us that exercise must be for Allah's pleasure, and he familiarised us with many of the Ahlulbayt (ams)'s teachings. I recited Ziyarah Ashura for the first time with Ibrahim. His view of this Ziyarah was different from the others. He considered Ziyarah Ashura as a daily salute of a soldier to his commander. He considered himself a soldier of the army of Ashura.

Before, when we wanted to laugh, we would tease someone and everyone would laugh, but when Ibrahim wanted to joke, he would leave everyone in fits. However, he would never mock anyone. He would remind us to laugh with each other, not at each other. In the beginning days of the war, it was Ibrahim who described spirituality and even changed the description of martyrdom for us. Ibrahim taught us how to live correctly.

These days, we witness that the youth in Tehran require a single cultural leader. There was a time when the youth of Tehran would accept a role model like Haj Hemmat[26] and they would look at him as a legend, but now, some of yesterday's soldiers follow the right path in the political issues, some follow the wrong path and some take a neutral stance. These people had great potential to create a cultural revolution in Tehran, but I say from my own experiences that if Ibrahim was among us with his special

---

26 Haj Ibrahim Hemmat was a commander of the Iranian military during the war and was martyred in March 1984 in Majnoon Island, Iraq

characteristics, he would have been our cultural, social, religious and revolutionary leader, and I have a reason for this.

I came to Tehran once again in 1981 and Ibrahim was recovering from his wounds. I attended many of the martyrs' funerals with Ibrahim. I had seen many times that some revolutionary youth would fall in love with Ibrahim's *akhlaq* and behaviour on their first meeting with him. When Ibrahim would go somewhere, he was always surrounded. Even people who weren't revolutionary were attracted to his loveable *akhlaq*. I had witnessed that during the martyrs' funerals, some of the commanders of Tehran would lecture and even make political stances. Ibrahim would normally speak with the commander or lecturer after the programme and carefully break down, examine, and analyse the words of that person and show him his problems. Once, he made one of the commanders understand that he had strayed away from God-wariness in his speech in the most beautiful manner possible. He said that you must be careful as you are a role model for the revolutionary youth. At that moment, I said to my friends, "Ibrahim's morals and sincere *akhlaq* attracts everyone to him, even people who aren't on the path of the Revolution. Most of our friends and even the youth follow Ibrahim. This person can be a leader for the revolutionary youth; he can even help them on a political level."

THE YA MAHDI (AJ) HEADBAND

Narrator: Hosein Rastegar-Nejad

I was friends with Ibrahim in our neighbourhood before the Revolution and we would play football and volleyball together. After the beginning of the war, I was informed that Ibrahim had gone to the warfront in the west of the country. In the middle of March 1981, I was dispatched to the city of Shush with a group

of videographers. The al-Mahdi (aj) Brigade under the commandership of Agha Ali Fazli was transferred to an area on the outskirts of the city of Shush by the name of Rofaeiyeh. In the days leading up to the Iranian New Year, the line-breaker troops of this brigade were going to begin the next stage of the operation. Meanwhile, we were busy filming the forces participating in the operation. The battalions entered the province one after the other under the darkness of the night. Everyone was praying that the enemy's lines would be broken because the enemy had put up a stubborn resistance the days before.

After a session of supplication and mourning, the line-breaker troops started to advance. I will never forget that night. We were hearing good news one after the other and the enemy's line had been broken. We were waiting for daybreak to get to the warfront of the fighting to film the heroics of our soldiers. When the sun rose, we advanced with some of the commanders. We had our cameras and journalist equipment. When I reached the warfront of fighting, my eyes fell upon one of the wounded soldiers. I unconsciously left my work and ran towards him. He was one of the line-breaker troops of the operation who had been wounded strangely. I knew him well; he was my old friend, Ibrahim, Ibrahim Hadi.

He wasn't able to speak properly as a bullet had entered through his mouth and come out from his neck. A bullet had also hit the back of his foot. Normally, when a bullet comes out from the back of the neck, it would wound either the spinal cord or jugular vein and the person's chances of survival would be slim, but Ibrahim was healthy and joyful. Some of the soldiers were gathered around him and everyone was speaking of his valour and heroism;

how he took an RPG in his hands the night before, destroyed the enemy tanks one by one and opened the way for the rest. I turned to Ibrahim and noticed that part of the hair above his head was burnt. You could see the path of a bullet in his hair. I exclaimed, "Ibrahim, what happened to your head?" He put his hand on his head and said with a mouth that could barely open, "Do you know why the bullet didn't dare to enter my head?" I asked why and he smiled and answered with difficulty, "The bullet was ashamed to enter my head as I had tied a Ya Mahdi (aj) headband on my head."

Ibrahim had also been wounded in the previous stage of the operation and as he had been wounded for the second time, he would have to go back, but he didn't want to. The medic bandaged his wounds and insisted that this stage of the operation had been successful and therefore, they sent him back with the rest of the wounded. Now that I think of Operation Fath ol-Mubin, I regret the fact that I didn't film or take pictures of those moments.

THE MIRACLE

Narrator: Hosein Jahanbakhsh

It was the beginning of April 1982 and my friends told me that Ibrahim was a patient in Najmiyyeh Hospital, so I went to visit him. My friendship with Ibrahim went back further than anyone else's. I owned a Volkswagen and a van which Ibrahim would use whenever he needed a vehicle. We were very easy-going with each other and therefore, I stayed in the hospital for a few hours so that I could help him if he needed anything. The management of the hospital was unable to do anything because of Ibrahim's friends. He had so many friends that they would come in groups and leave, and they didn't give any thought to the visiting times.

As I was sitting next to Ibrahim, one of the nurses came, touched a scarf on his face and left. When he noticed my surprise, he said, "This wounded man is a miracle. He has been cured and I wanted to bless my scarf." The nurse left and I asked Ibrahim,

"What's going on here? What was this nurse talking about? Also, why are all the other wounded soldiers coming to visit you from different sections of the hospital?" Ibrahim smiled and answered, "He's telling the truth. A miracle did occur. On the last night of the operation, I was near the Rofaeiyeh Bridge and it was the last stage of the operation. I had gone forward to destroy the trench of a soldier with a machine gun who was putting up strong resistance. It was dark as it was late at night. I threw a grenade close to the trench but to no avail. I went closer and threw the second grenade. I wanted to go around the back of the enemy's trench, but at that moment, an Iraqi officer came out and saw me to his left. The Iraqi officer had a weapon in his hand and asked in Arabic, "Who are you?" I replied in Arabic, "I'm one of you," but I felt that he doubted me. Before I could do anything, he brought his weapon up and started to shoot. When he aimed at me, I jumped to the ground. A bullet stroked the hair on my head, one bullet hit me in the ankle, and another went through my lip, broke one of my teeth and came out through my neck." I exclaimed, "From your neck?! Wasn't your jugular vein or spinal cord wounded?" Ibrahim smiled and said, "These doctors say that this is the miracle. The bullet hit the bones in my spinal cord." He continued, "Let me tell you the rest of the story. When I fell onto the floor, my whole body went numb! There was no feeling in my body. It was as if I had been electrocuted. I was alive and in good spirits, but however much I tried, I wasn't able to move my hands or legs. The Iraqi officer walked past and he was sure that he had killed me from the blood that was on my face. In those moments, I realised that the bullet had wounded my neck and as I was unable to move, I thought that my spinal cord had been severed. I spoke to Allah in my heart and said, "O' Allah, I wouldn't wish to be disabled. Leave my body healthy to serve Your servants, but only of course, if you see it fit. If it is your will for me to be disabled, I am surrendered to Your will." A few minutes passed in this state and I was continuously praising Allah and calling Lady Fatimah (a) in my heart. I also asked the Mother of the Masters for her intercession. After laying immobile on the floor for several minutes, the bleeding ceased. In those moments, I felt that I could move my foot. I slowly mobilised my foot over the ground and I then realised that I could once again feel my fingers. I opened and closed them. It was unbelievable! After fifteen minutes of trying, I wasn't able to move at all, but now, it had all changed. I thanked Allah. I dragged my hand across the floor and I felt the sling of my weapon. I slowly dragged the weapon towards myself as the weapon's sling was tied around my chest. The Iraqi officer was still preventing our soldiers from passing with his machine gun a few metres away from me. When he noticed me, I shot him dead and as the Iraqi officer had been killed, the rest of the people inside the trench fled. It took a few minutes for our soldiers to reach the trench and they saw me in that state and sent me back. Even though a bullet had hit my face and come out through my neck, I was in a good state and didn't feel any weakness in myself. I wanted to continue, but our work in that region succeeded. Here in Najmiyyeh Hospital, all the doctors say that this is a miracle. The bullet hit the bones of my spinal cord, but my spinal cord is in fine working order. They say that in all situations resembling mine, the wounded person would be paralysed, but it isn't the same for me." Of course, Ibrahim's ankle was badly wounded and kept him away from the warfront for six months.

I remember that a month later, Ibrahim came to Imam Sadiq (a) Art School in Province 12 of Tehran with Javad Afrasyabi and Mostafa Taqvaei to meet me. Ibrahim inquired, "Why is the school empty?" I replied, "They've brought a martyr. Shaheed Ghamkhar was the first student from this school to be martyred. They've now taken his body to the stands, but we don't have a reciter. Ibrahim, Allah has sent you." He quickly came, took the microphone, and started. You can't imagine what kind of majlis had begun. He was reciting, the people replying with their tears. He then recited a couplet of poetry and everybody started to whisper with him:

> *Mahdi, O' Mahdi, by the right of your mother Zahra,*
> *Tonight, confirm our victory!*

They started to move the body while reciting this poem. The crowd left the school and Agha Ibrahim got ready to leave with his friends. He said to me, "Hosein, look over here." He then sat in the middle of the school's playground and showed me the area of his stitches behind his neck. I felt it with my hand and there was a hole which had been stitched up right where the bones of his spinal cord were situated. I truly understood why the doctors had said that a miracle had occurred!

SPIRITUALITY

Narrator: Hosein Jahanbakhsh

Ibrahim would pay attention to the smallest issues which we wouldn't pay attention to. He would never waste and would help Allah's creation in whichever manner he could. He would use every moment of his life in the best way. I remember that we were sitting with each other behind the Sadri Gym. A small piece of dry bread had fallen beside Ibrahim. He picked up the bread and stated, "Look at how they disrespect Allah's blessings!" It was very hard and stale. He then took a stone and started to grind the bread as we were sitting in the stands. When he had ground the bread, he spread it at the end of one of the streets and a few minutes later, pigeons started to gather. The birds started to eat the food which Ibrahim had prepared for them.

I can say with courage that Ibrahim wouldn't even hurt an ant despite his strong body. I have just remembered a story as I mentioned ants. One day, we were going to the gym from home. I went a little ahead and then I looked back and saw Ibrahim was standing a little further behind me. He then crouched, looked around him and stood once more. I inquired, "What happened, Ibrahim?" He answered, "This place is full of ants. I wasn't paying attention and I put my foot right in the middle of the ants. I sat to see where the ants weren't travelling so that I could move." Ibrahim jumped over to my side of the street and we carried on walking. I said, "You're a strange person! We're getting late, but you're standing idle because of ants?!" He said, "These are also Allah's creation. If I had time, I would put out a handful of wheat for them, let alone crush them under my feet."

Whenever he noticed that one of his friends had a problem, he would put himself into hardship to resolve that person's problem. He thought of others' problems as his own. One of the youths from our gym became a supporter of the hypocrites after the Revolution, and Ibrahim was very sad because of this. He would constantly say, "Why did he become like this? Lest it was due to something I did!" He also struggled a lot to bring him back, but it didn't happen. On the other hand, one of the youths by the name of (Shaheed) Reza Munesan joined the military after the Revolution and grew spiritually. You can't imagine how happy Ibrahim was. He would always praise Shaheed Reza.

One of Ibrahim's other characteristics was that he never behaved badly with people. His complete *akhlaq* was good, calculated and well-wishing. He would never say no if someone asked him for something. He loved to attract people's hearts towards himself and he would do whatever he could to resolve people's problems.

I remember that we had gone to Inqilab Street together and he picked up two suitable pieces of wood to make weights from them. He then gave the wood to a carpenter close to Qiyam

Square so that he could craft them for him. After a while, when they were ready, he came to the gym and began to exercise. His weights were very heavy and lifting them were very difficult, but Ibrahim would exercise with them comfortably. He even held them in his hands in a horizontal manner for a few minutes. It would put pressure on any kind of person, but Ibrahim did this with ease. One of our friends asked Ibrahim, "Can you give those weights to me?" Ibrahim replied, "Ok, they're yours, but wait until tomorrow." After exercise, I said, "Ibrahim, you struggled so much to make those weights and now you want to give them away so easily?" He replied, "No problem. This person is a Sayyid and one of the children of the Holy Prophet (s)." At that time, I had a pair of weights which looked like Ibrahim's weights but lighter. Ibrahim gave me his weights and took mine and said, "This person won't be able to use my weights, they're too heavy. For this reason, I will give him your weights which look like mine."

One of Ibrahim's other characteristics was knowing his limits. He knew when and where to do something. He was even careful to not disrespect anyone when joking. Everybody respected him. Ibrahim would always forgive the shortcomings of others and he said to me many times, "Live and make friends in a way that people respect you. Don't ask people for things for no reason. Have self-respect." He would say, "Look at these domestic problems and fights. Most of them are because they don't have good *akhlaq*. This world isn't worth all the importance you give it! If a person can do something for Allah in this world, only then does this world hold value." When I got married, he indirectly advised me. He spoke like an experienced person and said, "In your life, if some problems arise which are hard for you to bear, keep it to yourself and don't let them bring you down. Ask Allah to resolve your problems."

FAJR IN CONGREGATION
Narrator: The martyr's friends

We were on our way to the warfront from Tehran. Ibrahim and I were travelling to Kermanshah in a personal vehicle. It was midnight and we still hadn't reached Kermanshah. I noticed that Ibrahim would constantly wake up and look at his watch. I asked him curiously, "Agha Ibrahim, what happened?" He replied, "Fajr is at four o'clock in the morning in Kermanshah. I want to pray my Fajr on time." A few minutes later, he woke up again. He stayed awake and asked if we could stop in front of one of the cafés. We prayed Fajr in congregation and on time, and then we set off again with our minds at rest.

In the summer of 1982, Ibrahim was in Tehran. Every day, we would go to different places together. At that time, Ibrahim would always be trying to resolve the problems of others. One night, we went to a majlis together and after that, we sat with the revolutionary youth. At midnight, he started to speak to the youth from our neighbourhood, and he was indirectly advising them. It was almost two o'clock in the morning and I was exhausted, as was Ibrahim. I had been working since the morning. I said, "I'm going home to sleep. What are you going to do?" Ibrahim replied, "I'm not going home. I'm scared I may fall asleep and miss my Fajr. You can go if you want." He then looked around himself. There was an empty fridge box on the floor at the end of the road. Ibrahim picked up the large box and went to Mohammadi Mosque. The entrance of the mosque was around two metres wide. Ibrahim put the box at the entrance of the mosque and laid there. He then said, "The adhan of Fajr is in two hours. The people who come to pray congregational prayers have to wake me up to get through." He then said gleefully, "This way, I won't miss my prayers and I will get to pray in congregation," and he fell asleep there comfortably. This was very strange for me. I couldn't understand why Ibrahim was so careful about Fajr. Even when he was a teenager, he would go to

Salman Mosque to pray Fajr in congregation.

Years after, I thought about how Ibrahim would behave towards Fajr prayers many times. Every night, we sit in front of the television spending hours watching films and football without paying any attention to the time of Fajr, and then we claim to follow the ways and customs of the martyrs! Later, I read somewhere that a man went to Imam Sadiq (a) and said, "I have committed a grave sin. What should I do?" The Imam (a) stated, "Even if it is greater than a mountain, Allah shall forgive it." The man replied, "It is greater than a mountain," and he told the Imam (a) what sin he had committed. He had committed a great sin, but Imam Sadiq (a) replied, "I thought that you had [purposely] missed your Fajr, but that's all you had done?!"

O' FATIMAH ZAHRA (A)!

Narrator: Hosein Jahanbakhsh and others

Ibrahim was well-versed in Islamic issues since we were together in the gym at a time when we didn't know much about religion. He loved all the Ahlulbayt (ams), but he had a special love for Lady Zahra (a). Whenever he would say her name, he would immediately say 'peace be upon her' afterwards. I remember once, the head of the gym started to recite poems about the calamities that befell Lady Fatimah (a) in memory of her death anniversary. While Ibrahim was doing push-ups, he started to cry very loudly. The others and I couldn't understand why Ibrahim was crying like that. A few moments later, his voice became louder and he started wailing. Eventually, our exercise was disrupted for a few minutes and the head of the gym started to recite different poems. If someone is like this while exercising in the gym, imagine what state they must be in when they attend a majlis where the calamities that befell Lady Zahra (a) are being mentioned! Ibrahim's love for Lady Fatimah (a) increased after Operation Fath ol-Mubin when he witnessed the several miracles that had occurred from her intercession.

The day Ibrahim was discharged by Najmiyyeh Hospital and we brought him home, eight of his friends were at his house. His mother and sisters were also at home. Ibrahim said, "Put a curtain up in the middle of the room so the women can come as well. I want to recite about the calamities that befell Lady Zahra (a)." He recited with a great pain in his voice and tears were flowing from his eyes. You can't imagine what kind of atmosphere he created with only those few people!

Whenever Ibrahim would return from the warfront on leave, he would visit me and borrow my Volkswagen. He would then go to Behesht-e Zahra with a group of his friends from the mosque. Ibrahim would always visit Behesht-e Zahra whenever he would return on leave. On time, I was blessed to be able to accompany them. There were thirteen of us crammed in the back of the van. When we got there, we would pass through the sectors with Ibrahim. It was as if he knew all the martyrs! He would tell us memories from the lives of the martyrs while we were walking. Whenever we would walk through a whole sector, he would turn to the Qibla and recite a short eulogy for Lady Fatimah (a) on behalf of the martyrs buried there or he would recite a few couplets of a poem, and make everyone cry. He would then say, "The reward belongs to the martyrs in this sector." We would then visit the next sector.

He would never talk about himself. He would never say the word 'I', but towards the end, he would speak less. I felt his mind was elsewhere. In these last few months, especially in autumn of 1982, whenever we would go somewhere and ask Ibrahim to recite, he would immediately start to recite about the calamities which befell Lady Zahra (a) and then he would lose consciousness.

THE GOOD OLD DAYS

Narrator: The martyr's sister

I can't talk about Ibrahim, it's very difficult for me. Whenever I remember his short time with us, I become upset and anxious. The golden era of our family was when he was with us, but being separated from him destroyed our lives. I ask for Allah's help to introduce a part of his spirituality and characteristics to Ibrahim's new friends.

My time with Ibrahim was short but educational. Not only was he a brother to me but also a teacher and guide. He would train us through his *akhlaq*. He would do whatever he needed to do on time. He had a schedule in his life. When he wanted to teach his brother or sister something, he wouldn't just advise and speak to them. First, he would teach, mostly indirectly, and then he would accompany the person to see the result. Ibrahim first worked on his family to encourage *amr bil ma'ruf* and hijab before anyone else. He taught us how to do *amr bil ma'ruf* correctly through his actions. I remember once, he bought gifts, gave them to me and said, "Give these to your friends who have recently started to pray and wear the hijab." He did this forty years ago, a time when nobody paid attention to these issues!

He was such a beloved personality in our lives that we would accept whatever he said immediately. If he told us to wear a chador, we would do so without question, but he would also tell us why we should do so. When we wanted to leave the house, he would say in a friendly manner, "The chador is a sanctuary for a woman, a fort and a supporter. Protect this sanctuary well." He would present his argument in a way that we would accept them with all our heart. Once when I was young, I wanted to go out wearing colourful socks. Ibrahim said to me, "A woman's sanctity is protected by the chador. Now, if you wear colourful socks, you will attract attention and the sanctuary of the chador will be destroyed. Colourful socks attract the attention of *non-mahrams*." He would say, "If women observe the limits of interaction with the opposite gender, you will notice families will live more comfortably. Speaking loudly in front of the opposite gender sets the foundation for corruption and sin. If the limits are observed, the opposite gender wouldn't dare to do anything." He would often say, "Respect the hijab as it protects your comfort and is the best kind of *amr bil ma'ruf* for you."

Ibrahim gave a lot of importance to guests and serving them. He would prepare the best for his guest, but he hated showing off. He would say, "If we want to all coexist comfortably, we must not show off. We shouldn't put ourselves to trouble when inviting others for food. We must entertain guests and interact with our families according to the commands of the religion and without showing off so that family relations can stay intact."

He was always the first to do something good. He enjoyed doing things for Allah's pleasure from morning to night. He had a small notebook which he would use to write down what he did during the day. He would be more joyful than ever on a day in which he did a lot of work in the way of Allah. I remember he once said to me, "Today is the best day of my life. Allah blessed me and I was able to resolve many of His servants' problems." He would never become overjoyed when he got something material. None of the worldly attachments would make him happy. Nothing would please him except if he made another person happy in the way of Allah. He wouldn't wear new clothes and he would say, "I will wear new clothes once everyone can afford to wear them." He had these traits even before the Revolution. In the days of the Revolution, he would do things that would break his *nafs*. For example, when the people didn't have oil due to strikes, Ibrahim would carry large barrels of oil and visit people's houses. I even saw Ibrahim driving a wagon full of oil barrels. He was pushing the wagon through the roads and streets to give the people their oil.

During the days of the Revolution, we were very worried about him as he would come home very late. He would shout *'Allahu*

Akbar' loudly on the rooftops with his friends. Each moment, we could hear the shooting getting closer and we would get nervous. One night, he was later than usual, and a curfew was in place. Suddenly, someone started banging on the door loudly. As soon as I opened the door, Ibrahim ran into the house, followed by a bullet! He said very calmly, "The soldier aimed well, but his bullet missed the target!"

One of his greatest desires was that one day in the Islamic Republic, everyone would leave their work when it was time for prayers, recite the adhan and go to pray and speak to Allah, meaning when Allah calls them towards himself, everyone would be busy in worship. He would always go to the mosque to pray and if he couldn't go to the mosque, he would perform congregational prayers at home. He had a small comb in his pocket which he would use to comb his hair and beard at the time of prayers and would prepare himself to speak to his Lord.

You may have heard that on an intelligence operation, Ibrahim carried a wounded Iraqi captive on his back and brought him back to the Iranian forces. When he gave him over to the soldiers, he had a severe stomach-ache and they had to operate on his appendix in hospital. The doctor asked him, "Why did you do that? You shouldn't have travelled this long way in the mountainous terrain like that," but he replied, "I needed to, nobody was able to take him back, he was wounded." No one told us, but when he returned to Tehran after a while, I saw a few medical photos in his luggage. When I asked him why, he was forced to tell me what happened.

However, his personality had completely changed the last time we were together in Tehran. Some days, he wouldn't eat food. When we would complain, he would say, "I must prepare this body!" On the cold winter nights, he would sleep without a blanket or a mattress. Again, when we complained about this, he would say, "I must prepare this body! It must get used to long rest in the dust!" I remember my last farewell with him well. He was never like this; he kept himself to himself. Before Operation Before the Dawn, he came to our house on a motorcycle and said, "I'm going, pray I don't return!" When he saw I was worried, he continued, "This community still hasn't united. I don't know why they're like this! I don't want anything from this world, not even a handful of its dust. I want to take revenge for the slap of Lady Fatimah (a). If I'm worthy and Allah accepts me, I want my body to be torn apart and my soul to rest in Lady Zahra (a)'s vicinity."

AMRIYYEH

Narrator: Mortaza Parsaeiyan

I was working at the IRGC headquarters in Tehran towards the end of February 1983. One day, they told me somebody was there to see me at the door. I went and to my surprise, it was Ibrahim. You can't imagine how happy I was. We went inside together. Many of my friends either knew him or had heard of him. He stayed for lunch after I insisted. Of course, I told him that I would pay for the food and he wouldn't have to worry about taking someone else's rights. I asked him, "Dash Ibrahim, what brings you here?" He replied, "I want you to get me an Amriyyeh so I can go to the South." At that time when the baseejis who were going to the warfront wanted to be dispatched somewhere, they needed a personal letter called an Amriyyeh.

At lunchtime, we went to the dining hall. That year, there was a strange atmosphere and no one would laugh in our department. Everyone would sit with buttoned collars and religious appearances. They thought that these things increase sincerity and God-wariness. When Ibrahim came to the dining hall, he asked me, "By the way, I heard you got married, right?" I replied, "Yes, Insha'Allah you must come to my wedding and recite." Before I completed my sentence, Ibrahim suddenly slapped the table and said, "May Allah bless you!" He then recited a couplet of poetry and started laughing and slapping the table. When I saw the people around us staring, I became very embarrassed and said, "Agha Ibrahim, this is wrong, the IRGC commanders have come here today and are sitting in the hall." Ibrahim signalled with a movement of his head, "I know, I'm doing this on purpose!" I didn't understand, but he disrupted the dining hall quite a lot on that day.

That evening, I went to Ibrahim's house with his Amriyyeh and train ticket. He was ecstatic. I told him to go to the railway station the next day and to go to the south via the train to Ahwaz. I told him I would join him soon.

The day after, I went to the director of my department and asked him many times to give me a few days of leave so I could go to the South. Everybody had heard of the operation taking place. He didn't agree, but I insisted so much that he agreed a few days later. I managed to reach the South as the operation began. There, I heard that Ibrahim was meant to advance with the spies so I was with him for a short time. It was as if he was in his own world! He was extremely different, and he then left on his own. I saw Mahdi Khandan, Hashem Kalhor and some of my other friends and I joined the Meqdad Battalion with them. We started to work with the Meqdad Battalion, and we reached the Doqolu Mountains, but we were forced to retreat when the order was given and I was unable to meet him for the last time.

One of my friends said, "The day Ibrahim came to the warfront for the last time, he said to me, 'This is the end, I don't want anyone to speak about me anymore.' He then continued calmly, 'As if no one has even heard of Ibrahim Hadi. I don't want anyone to speak about me, nothing. I don't want to take up even a handful of dust. I don't want them to have a funeral for me or speak of me, nothing!' My heart sunk when I heard how Ibrahim spoke, but I didn't say anything. Ibrahim had said this and left. This truly happened. Twenty-five years passed and no one spoke of Ibrahim, no programme, no shrine, but when Allah wishes to give respect to someone and elevate his status, no one can stop His will. In 2015, there were more than twenty martyrdom anniversary programmes for Agha Ibrahim because of the contact that had been established with the Shaheed Hadi Group. In one case, someone from Yazd contacted us and said, 'I have made an oath with the martyr and held a majlis in his memory. The lecture and recitations were beautiful, and we served dinner to a thousand people. Allah knows how blessed this gathering was!'"

The final time Ibrahim went to the warfront, Operation Before the Dawn was about to begin, and there was great excitement beforehand. The final coordination meeting of the commanders took place in Dehlavieh and each commander went to the meeting with one of the baseeji soldiers of their division. Haj Hemmat loved Ibrahim Hadi, so he sent a message to Hosein Allah-Karam and told him to bring Ibrahim Hadi so he could recite Dua Tawassul after the meeting.

The meeting began and the baseejis, most of whom were acting as drivers for their commanders, sat outside the meeting hall. An hour later, they brought dinner. Dishes of bread and kebab went into the meeting but they brought bread and potatoes for the baseejis. Ibrahim Hadi was meant to go to the meeting hall after dinner to recite Dua Tawassul, but whilst the commanders were eating dinner, they heard Dua Tawassul being recited outside. Ibrahim had started to recite the Dua with the *baseejis*! After dinner, Ibrahim wouldn't agree to recite Dua Tawassul for the commanders despite their insistence. He said, irritated, "I've read my Dua." The meeting finished and everyone got ready to go back to their bases and headquarters.

Haj Hosein narrates, "When we got into the car and left, I gave a box to Ibrahim and said, 'I've brought you some bread and kebab.' Whilst driving, Ibrahim took the bread and kebab from me and threw it out the window with his other hand! He then said, 'I ate bread and potatoes with the other baseejis. Let the desert animals eat this food!' I didn't say anything. A few moments later, Ibrahim said, 'We are all baseejis. I'm frightened of the day the baseejis and the commanders eat different foods. That day, it will be difficult to keep working!'" The next day, the final coordination was completed and the brigades of the Hazrate Rasool (s) Division started to move towards the southern bases of Fakkeh.

INSIDE THE TRENCH

Narrator: One of the survivors from the trench

In Operation Before the Dawn, Ibrahim advanced with the Kumayl Brigade and after much struggle, they reached the second trench in Fakkeh, a trench later known as the Kumayl Trench. The several days of siege had drained the energy of the forces. The commanders and vice-commanders of the brigade had also been martyred. The only person who was able to organise the forces from an aspect of physical strength and military experience was Ibrahim. From here on in, I will narrate from one of the survivors of this brigade:

When we were under siege, Ibrahim Hadi had to do something to boost the morale of his companions as he was the only person able to take the reins of commandership. He first ordered the healthy troops to spread out over a 400-metres to guard the trench. Every two soldiers made cover on the edge of the trench twenty metres away from each other and stationed themselves there. He asked the troops only to shoot at the enemy when they were exactly in the range of fire because of the lack of ammunition. He then went to a few people who were healthier and physically stronger than the others and asked them to gather the barbed wire from the end of the trench. At the end of the trench, there were a few lines of circular barbed wire. Doing so without any kind of equipment was very difficult for the soldiers.

Ibrahim's next task was to separate the martyrs from the wounded and the soldiers inside the trench. There was a part of the trench a short distance away from the soldiers which was not in view because the trench turned at the end. The soldiers carried the bodies of the martyrs there with great difficulty. Carrying the bodies wasn't difficult itself, but rather having to separate from their friends made the work difficult and mentally exhausting. A heavy sorrow had settled on the hearts of the soldiers. Some of the soldiers were close to dying just on this short journey. These lions who would valorously fight the enemy couldn't even move the bodies of their martyred friends! I remember nobody spoke to each other. Only tears trickled down from their eyes. The eyes of the soldiers were sewn to the calm and oppressed faces of their martyred friends. Tears trickled down from their eyes onto their pale and dusty cheeks and would fall to the ground. The fond memories we shared with the martyrs didn't spare us a moment of calmness. Now they were carrying the noble bodies of their friends on their shoulders with sorrow and regret and taking them to a place so they wouldn't have to see them. Sadness and sorrow had overcome their entire existence.

After moving the martyrs to the end of the trench, we now had to find a safe place for the wounded. There were many wounded soldiers in the trench. Some had lost their arms and legs while the insides of some other soldiers had fallen out after being hit by bullets and shrapnel. Ibrahim was looking for someplace to put the wounded where they would be safe from the shrapnel of the missiles occasionally fired into the trench. The only place that came to his mind was the walls of the trench which had been damaged by missiles. Ibrahim asked the soldiers to dig at the walls with their bayonets and create parapets.[27] The soldiers got to work immediately and an hour later, we had made cover to keep the wounded safe with great difficulty.

Now, the trench had returned to a somewhat normal state. I looked at the soldiers carefully. I saw no sign of weakness or fright in the faces of the Ali Akbars[28] of Khomeini (ra). Yes, this was the second trench. This is the same place where the divine angels watched the soldiers of the Holy Prophet (s) and Amir al-Mu'mineen (a) in the end of times. This is a place which was a ladder to the heavens. This is the place which would later be known as the Kumayl Trench.

Ibrahim jumped at the sound of an explosion. He went out the trench and assessed the area of the Doqolu Mountain behind us. He then called a few people who had experience in operations. When they came, he said, "In order for us to retreat, go to the first trench and from there, return to our troops, we have no choice but to leave the wounded. After leaving the trench, the healthy troops must crawl through four hundred metres of minefields and barbed wire. If they survive the explosion of the mines, the deathly fire of the artillery guns, the sentry guns, and the enemy's machine guns, only then will they reach the first trench. After passing the first trench, they must crawl for another seven hundred metres to reach

---

27   A protective wall or earth defence along the top of a trench or other place of concealment for troops

28   Ali Akbar was the son of Imam Husayn (a) who stayed at his side despite suffering from severe hunger and thirst until he was martyred on the 10th of Muharram in the land of Karbala. This is an example to show how loyal they were to Imam Khomeini (ra) as if they were his sons.

the Doqolu Mountains. They then have to quickly run for a further two hundred metres to reach the backside of the mountains. One side of these mountains is occupied by the enemy and the other side belongs to our soldiers. You must be careful of the enemy's fire as they are on top of the mountains." After this, he added, "Go and brief the healthy troops." According to what Ibrahim said, once you reached the mountain, there was hope in survival, but only people who were nimble and healthy could go this way, not people who had been hungry, thirsty and sleepless for the last four days, not to mention they had been fighting the enemy under the most difficult mental and psychological circumstances.

Ibrahim went to ask the wounded how they are and reassure them. Whenever he would pass a wounded soldier, he would sit next to him for a few moments, caress him and speak with him. I would stay next to him. He walked a few metres forward and sat with a two-person group. One was a young teenager leaning against the wall of the trench and the other was sleeping calmly in his friend's lap. Ibrahim sat next to him and the teenager got up slightly in respect of Ibrahim. Ibrahim asked him how his friend was, and the teenager said quietly but firmly, "My friend answered Allah's call a few moments ago," and gently caressed his face and hair. Ibrahim looked at him with amazement, then he bent over and kissed the martyr's dusty and bloodstained cheeks. It was as if he had no energy to get up again. Tears started to flow from Ibrahim's eyes. He then carefully lifted the martyr's body and laid it alongside the other pure bodies of the martyrs. Ibrahim came back and hugged that teenager.

The young soldier said, "My friend and I were together since we were children and we went to school together. When the war began, we left school with great hardship and came to the warfront. They put us in this brigade, the Kumayl Brigade. Before this operation, our brigade was on the defensive lines for eighteen days in the province of Fakkeh. We even managed to take eleven enemy soldiers captive there. When the operation finished, they brought the brigade back so that they could send us to Dokouheh for rest and then we could go on leave from there. When we were getting ready to go to Dokouheh in the morning, the commander gathered us all and said, "There are plans for an operation in this province and the commander of the division has asked us to take part in the operation as we are ready for battle. The Imam is waiting for the result of this operation. So, if you aren't tired, let's be the troops to break the enemy's front line in this operation." Even though many of the soldiers were tired as they were forced to sleep in the deserts of Chinaneh without any equipment for two nights and were counting the moments until they could see their families, the thought of pleasing the Imam (ra) was a whole different subject altogether. All the soldiers agreed to participate in this operation as the forces that would break the enemy's front line. Some of the forces took their bath of martyrdom with cold water in the cold winter weather and got ready for the operation. We then joined the operation." Ibrahim was listening carefully to the words of this teenager and a strange silence dominated over the province.

THE SORROWFUL DAYS

The only sound that would break the mysterious silence of the trench was the sound of Ibrahim's recitations. He would rejuvenate his fatigued companions with his beautiful voice. Ibrahim's whispers were a source of comfort amongst all the blood, wounds, thirst, and hunger. This reminder of the calamities which befell our mother and her broken ribs gave the companions of the trench the ability to fly. With his voice, the trench came back to life. When Ibrahim would recite the adhan, those who had some energy left in their bodies would go to the wall of the trench so that they could get up by leaning on it and got ready to pray. In a more heavenly state, the wounded would turn themselves towards the Qibla with difficulty and would place their pale and bloody foreheads onto the dust of the trench as a sign of love and servitude. Truly, Allah takes pride in creating such humans to His angels! In the trench, (Shaheed) Sayyid Ja'far Taheri would recite the Holy Qur'an and even interpret it after prayers. When the soldiers would hear Sayyid Ja'far's beautiful voice reciting the Qur'an, their hearts would find comfort and they would be reassured in their rightfulness. Some of the soldiers who had pocket-sized Qur'ans would recite along with Sayyid Ja'far and their tears would silently flow from their eyes. A few others who had found a pen or pencil would look for anything they could write on and would write their wills.

Everyone was whispering duas in every corner of the trench and would cry out loud. Some were recite Dua Tawassul and some Ziyarah Ashura. Others would quietly recite eulogies and shed tears. We had a Sudanese captive in the trench. When he saw the soldiers reciting the Qur'an, he said in complete bewilderment and disbelief, "Do you also recite the Qur'an?! They told us we were going to fight the fire-worshippers!" When that captive was certain we were Muslim, he insisted to us that he wanted to be sent back. He was confessing that he had made a terrible mistake.

The soldiers would dig at the walls of the trench with their bayonets and even their hands and made stairs to climb up. They would sometimes climb the steps quickly and shoot at the Baathists to display their strength and keep the Iraqis from coming close to the trench. The Iraqi commandos had such large physiques and were so tall that anyone who saw them would become terrified. Whenever they wanted to advance against the Iranian forces, the enemy would concentrate its fire on the trench so that the commandos could easily come close to the trench. This bombardment made it difficult to shoot over the edge of the trench.

Sometimes, these lions of war would adopt an ingenious and self-sacrificing method to combat the commandos. Before the Baathists began their bombardment, they would voluntarily leave the trench and would advance more than sixty metres towards the enemies. They would then hide amongst the pure bodies of the martyrs and wait for the commandos to arrive. After that, they would shoot at the accursed people or throw grenades at them. They would kill them one by one or force them to retreat like this. They even took two other people captive using this method and brought them to the trench.

The enemy's bombardment had been repelled by the technique that our forces had adopted to defend the trench. It was undoubtedly the bravery which stemmed from the faith of the warriors of Islam which empowered them to make a whole brigade of seasoned and armed Baathist commandos retreat. Despite this, the Baathist bombardment had added to the number of martyrs and wounded soldiers. First aid was very difficult and ineffective because of the lack of medical equipment. The soldiers used their scarves to bandage their wounds and because there was even a lack of scarves, they were forced to use the scarves covering the bodies of the martyrs. Sometimes, a young teenager had to bandage the arm of a wounded soldier which was just hanging on by a small piece of flesh! The wounded were constantly crying out of the severity of thirst and were asking for water. The trench was constantly targeted by the enemy's missiles.

Once the enemies laid off the trench, Ibrahim sent a few soldiers to either side of the trench to gather all the troops. The soldiers quickly gathered around Ibrahim by the wall of the trench. By then, the soldiers who weren't wounded had reduced in number. Ibrahim said, "We can no longer stay in the trench. We must retreat to the Doqolu Mountains tonight however possible." He then continued, "As the trench is under siege and there are many obstacles between us and our forces, one veteran must travel with two other inexperienced soldiers as a group and crawl and retreat to the Doqolu Mountains." After designating the three-person groups, he asked the forces to return to their posts and to protect the trench and the wounded until nightfall. That day, there were almost seventy badly wounded people inside the trench who wouldn't be able to retreat. When the forces began to disperse, a young teenager asked Ibrahim a strange question, "Will the wounded also be able to come back with us? If we can't take them back, what will happen to them?!" Everyone was looking at each other, stunned. There was no answer to such a question. Ibrahim replied to that teenager, "You don't worry about the wounded, I will be with them." The teenager replied bravely, "Then I will also stay, and I will protect the wounded until the last drop of my blood." It was a difficult decision for the others to make. Four days of hunger, thirst, exhaustion, and siege hadn't spared them any energy. Another soldier from the corner of the trench said that he would also stay and suddenly, all the soldiers expressed their decision to stay with courage. Ibrahim said as if he was pleased with the soldiers' decision, "We will all stand like men and resist." He then paused for a bit and continued, "But brothers, perhaps nobody would be able to help us until the last moment. Have you thought of everything? We have no water, no food, no ammunition; martyrdom is just a step away. Are you ready?" It was as if our soldiers had been rejuvenated. Their self-sacrifice and chivalry filled the trench with affection and virtue. Everybody agreed to stay loyal to the promise they had made. Even those in the trench who had fewer injuries were not willing to retreat. They didn't want to leave the sick and wounded and were saying, "Disloyalty is not one of our values. We will remain here, and we will not move from here until we have taken the wounded back!"

WATER

There was a strange feeling had developed amongst the forces. Ibrahim said to the soldiers, "Now that you want to stay, we must ration the water, ammunition and anything we can eat in the trench until we decide what to do with the wounded." Within a few minutes, all the water flasks had been gathered at the end of the trench in front of Ibrahim. Some of the soldiers were able to gather rainwater from small holes with the lids of their flasks which were collected there from the rain over the previous nights and pour it into their flasks. This water was salty. The day before, one of the soldiers had filled his flask halfway up with this water, but he then realised that two Baathist bodies had fallen into the water. Some of the soldiers who would leave the trench at night and lie among the martyrs to ambush the enemy would bring back the flasks of their martyred allies to the trench. Some of the water belonged to the killed Iraqis, but most of this water was salty which was only used to wet the lips of the wounded. It was time to distribute the flasks, the flasks being few and the thirsty many. Agha Ibrahim's job had become very difficult as the Iraqi captives were also thirsty and looking at us with disappointment, but he had accounted for everybody, even the Baathist captives. He then looked at the few flasks. There was no need for complicated mathematical equations. There was such little water one would suffer from distress if he had to distribute it. Ibrahim had champion-like values. He gave each of the Baathist captives one flask. One of the soldiers complained to Ibrahim, but he said, "These are now our guests, us Iranians have a custom of giving our guest the best. The master of the youth of this universe put his captive and murderer before himself. How can our hearts beat with the love of Ali (a), but we don't have his values?!" Nobody objected to Ibrahim after that. They had learnt the lessons of forgiveness and self-sacrifice from the righteous school of the Imams (ams). Ibrahim then gave every three wounded soldiers one flask and every six healthy soldiers one flask.

Our soldiers were so virtuous that despite the heat of the day, fatigue, and extreme thirst, some of the healthy soldiers would leave their portion of the water and give it to the wounded. We also gathered some canned food. Every eight wounded soldiers received one can and the others didn't get any. The soldiers of the trench were fighting while oppressed with bloody and pale faces, dry skin, and chapped lips from thirst, and they didn't let even an ounce of fear to their hearts. The warriors of Kumayl resisted with all their might, but exhaustion and a lack of sleep had truly battered them. The enemy's bullets and the bombardments had dominated them. The enemy had even closed off the routes for supplies and reinforcements by using the tall mountains which were overlooking the trench to bombard the route.

The sun set and Ibrahim recited the adhan for Maghrib with a more comforting voice. The companions of Sayyid ash-Shuhada (a)[29] who had graduated from the school of Ashura arose once more to recite their prayers. Although their number was few and they weren't in a suitable condition, the soldiers still wanted to strike fear in the heart of the enemy. The only obstacle stopping them was that they didn't have suitable weapons or ammunition, and this had become the thorn in their sides. The only weapons we had were Kalashnikovs and two RPGs, both with very limited ammunition. Our ammunition was so limited that the soldiers would scour the floor to find a few bullet cartridges. There was also a sentry gun in the trench which had no bullets and was broken, rendering it useless. Over the past few days, we had RPGs and grenades in the trench and the soldiers would stop the enemy with this limited amount of ammunition, but now, they only had a few Kalashnikov bullet cartridges and a few RPG rockets which Ibrahim had ordered us to save for special circumstances.

Ibrahim summoned the soldiers who still had some energy and sent them secretly under the cover of night to search the

---

29   A title of Imam Husayn (a) meaning the Master of Martyrs

bodies of the martyrs and Baathists around the trench and to bring any ammunition, water or provisions they could find back to the trench. Some gave their lives in this way and never returned to the trench. Some would bring some water and ammunition and some others who had more energy even went extremely close to our forces to find ammunition or water. They could have easily returned to our troops and never come back to the trench, but these strong-willed forces had grounded themselves in the trench. Loyalty and virtue was mixed with their flesh and blood in a way that they would return to the trench once again with a few bullet cartridges they had found even after enduring great pain and would bear the difficulties. Sometimes when the soldiers would go out amongst the dead bodies to find ammunition, water, or provisions, they would witness harrowing scenes which would scar them for many years after. Many times, they had no choice but to search their martyred friends' bodies so that they could find some bullet cartridges or a flask of water. Other times, they would also see wounded people who had no arms or legs and were begging them for a sip of water. Such moments of shame were thorns in the side of the soldiers for many years after that and slowly reduced them to nothingness.

The winter nights of Fakkeh were cold and exhausting and the cold wintery breeze of the desert would trouble everybody. However, due to their bodies which were torn apart, the wounded were in more pain than the rest. The soldiers would try to protect the wounded from the cold to the best of their capability. Some would give their clothes to the wounded to wear. The cold weather was so bitter that one of the soldiers suggested to dig graves at the end of the trench, lay the wounded in there and cover them up to their necks so that they can stay warm. Now, the wounded people were inside the pits up to their necks. Their bodies had become numb due to severe bleeding and this seemed like the only way to keep them safe from the bitter winter cold. Some of the wounded resisted against the cold in this way and survived, but others never woke up from their sweet sleep. They quietly reached the peak of existence and flew towards their martyred allies.

It was an unequal battle. The peak of chivalry and compassion stood against the enemy's brutality and savagery. When the Iraqis would come into the battlefield with stretchers to take their wounded soldiers back, our soldiers gave them safety at the peak of chivalry so that they could take their wounded soldiers back, despite having a clear shot at them. These were the virtues of the Iranian soldiers. In contrast, an Iraqi sniper's favourite hobby was killing our half-dead and spiritless wounded soldiers who had fallen in the middle of the battlefield. The fourth night of siege slowly bade farewell to the soldiers. On one hand, the cruelty displayed on their friends' bodies didn't spare them a moment of comfort and on the other hand, thirst had spared them no strength. The desert of Fakkeh and its second trench recorded every little detail of what happened in those few nights.

I was with them and was sitting amongst the wounded in a corner of the trench, falling in and out of sleep. In these conditions, Ibrahim was our only beacon of joy. He was considered our superior. One of the soldiers made his way to Ibrahim with great difficulty. He looked at him and started to speak to him relatively loudly. Suddenly, I could no longer sleep, and I started to watch them. He said to Ibrahim, "I swear to God, nobody has been able to defeat us until now, neither the enemy nor its never-ending bombardment, but now, thirst has spared us no reprieve. If we just get a little bit of water, we will destroy the enemy." I don't know why, but I started to remember Karbala. I remembered when Ali Akbar (a) said to his father after returning from the battlefield, "Thirst is killing me." I remembered Imam Husayn (a)'s embarrassment. I knew that Ibrahim was thirstier than the others. That day when he distributed the water flasks, there was nothing left for him! Ibrahim lowered his head and thought in shame. He decided to leave the trench and do something about the thirst of the soldiers in whichever way possible. Right then at midnight,

Ibrahim left the trench and didn't speak to anyone out of shame. It was almost dawn and the sun was slowly rising. I was worried in case something had happened to Ibrahim. Everyone was upset as he was the only source of happiness in our lives. Suddenly, I saw someone jump down from the top of the trench, making everyone happy. Ibrahim had come back with a few flasks full of water. All the fighters and wounded soldiers were glad. I said to Ibrahim, "You were late, we got scared!" Ibrahim replied, "I went all the way, close to the Doqolu Mountains to find water and saw our troops fighting with the Baathists." I exclaimed, "You went all the way there?! Well..." Ibrahim got up and went to see the troops.

Every night, there was fighting on the Doqolu Mountains. The mountains changed hands several times between the Iranians and the Baathists. At night, the Iranian troops would attack, and the mountains would fall to the warriors of Islam, but in the daytime, the Baathists would reclaim it with a wide-ranging counterattack. Ibrahim had gone close to our troops and he could have never returned to the trench, but he had returned with a few flasks of water as well. What do we know? Perhaps he had not put his lips to the water, following the path of his master, Abbas (a) when he remembered the dry lips of the soldiers. The soldiers all envied his great soul and would praise him.

THE FINAL DAY

It was the sixth day of battle and our fifth day in the trench, coinciding with the 11th of February 1983. The Baathists increased their pressure, but the few soldiers left resisted. At noon, almost all our ammunition had finished. Ibrahim Hadi gathered the exhausted soldiers in a corner of the trench and briefed them, "Brothers, don't be upset. Now that you have decided to stay like men, even if we are all martyred, we are not alone. Rest assured that our

mother, Lady Fatimah (a), will come and visit us." The soldiers' eyes welled up with tears and trickled onto their cheeks. Ibrahim continued, "Don't be upset. Even if we are martyred in alienation, our mother won't leave us alone!" The soldiers who hadn't let extreme hunger, thirst and injury get to their minds at the least finally broke down and started to mourn. Everybody started to call out to our mother with weak voices and dry lips and were slapping their faces. When we started to remember the calamities which befell our mother, the Baathists paused their bombardment! The area was in complete silence and all you could hear was the sound of the soldiers shouting out to their mother from inside the trench. The soldiers had been under siege for five days in the trench. During this period, the sun during the day, the cold of the night, alienation, loneliness, injury, thirst, and hunger showed the patience of the supporters of Khomeini (ra). Soon, they would be spiritually annihilated in Allah's way. The soldiers stood and resisted.

Almost all the soldiers were wounded and there were no more scarves or undershirts left to bandage the wounds. The soldiers' wounds were gaping. The soldiers were cramped together and the enemy was determined to destroy the trench by tightening the siege and applying more pressure. First, the Baathist commandos attacked the soldiers of the Hanzaleh Brigade who were under siege in the third trench since the night before and after an hour of severe resistance, they massacred the soldiers. They then entered the Kumayl Trench from different directions. They were numerous and our soldiers had fired their last bullets. There was nothing left for us to resist with. One of the enemy commandos managed to go up out of the trench he shot towards the defenceless soldiers in the trench with his RPG. The RPG rocket exploded next to Sayyid Ja'far Taheri. His head and arm were severed from his body and fell a few metres back! Only a few days before, he had given his portion of water to an Iraqi captive, and now he gave his life with dry lips among the dust and blood. I remember Sayyid left the trench the same day before sunrise with six other soldiers. They laid amongst the bodies of the martyrs and waited for the commandos to come. When the commandos came, a severe battle broke out. Three warriors were martyred there and Sayyid Ja'far returned to the trench with two others.

Mohammad Shareef was another of the brave soldiers of the trench. He was fighting valorously. He was fatally wounded while fighting and at the moment of his martyrdom, he said to his friends, "Tell my mother to go to Shah Abdul-Azim and pray for me." He then raised his hand towards the skies and shouted with a shaky voice but in a mystical tone, "Mahdi dear (aj), take my hand!" The soldiers saw that when he finally achieved martyrdom, his innocent face opened with joy! He stared at a certain place and his eyes glistened.

We were all overwhelmed, and we were expecting the enemies to be over our heads at any moment. In these moments, we found out that the enemy had entered from the end of the trench. Ibrahim Hadi rushed towards the end of the trench and suddenly, several strong explosions came from the direction in which Ibrahim had run. Moments later, one of the soldiers from the end of the trench came running towards us and yelled, "Ibrahim has also been martyred!" The blood drained from my face and all the memories of the past few days went running through my mind.

I had lost all my hope. These were the last few moments of our soldiers' resistance in the trench and someone was able to contact the commanders via radio. He said, "Send our salaam to our Imam. Tell the Imam on our behalf that we resisted like Imam Husayn (a) just like he said, we stayed and fought till the last man."

Suddenly, we saw the barrels of the Iraqi weapons over our heads. The Iraqi commandos had reached our trench and hundreds of gun barrels were aiming towards us. An officer entered the trench with another Baathist soldier through the stairs. We were all laying on the floor wounded, and the officer looked at us. They had come to take revenge for the past few days from defenceless and wounded people. The Iraqi officer loaded his weapon and whenever he would walk past a soldier, he would make his life eternal with a single bullet. Moments later, the Iraqi officer left the trench and ordered the soldiers who were overlooking the trench to fire. They fired mercilessly at the trench and murdered the honourable children of Khomeini (ra) in cold blood.

The Iraqis finished off the trench close to noon on Friday, the 11th of February 1983. They would shoot at any moving thing in the trench and after making sure nothing was left alive in the trench, they moved their troops out of the area and went back. The trench had now become a slaughterhouse, full of bodies, drenched in blood and torn to pieces! There was complete silence in the trench and every now and then, the sound of the wind could be heard. An hour passed since the Iraqis left. My blood-drenched body had fallen next to the bodies of the martyrs, and perhaps that's why they didn't shoot me. I opened my eyes and the sunlight shined on them. I sat up with difficulty. My body was wounded and fatigued. I managed to get up with great difficulty, but I couldn't see any living creature around me. There was complete silence in the area. I looked at my surroundings and I noticed that one of the wounded soldiers was moving. Another person also stood up from amongst the wounded. Despite the brutal activities of the Baathists, a few of the soldiers had stayed safe from their bullets by Allah's grace.

We waited until it became dark and by that time, we were ten living people. We agreed to use the same method Ibrahim had told us about and return. When it became dark, a few soldiers from the Hanzaleh Brigade also joined us and we managed to take back some of the badly wounded soldiers with their help. These were the final moments and I helped everybody out through the steps at the end of the trench. I looked back inside the trench once again. The desecrated bodies of the martyrs were scattered all over. I don't know, I really don't know how to describe those five days. I should have gone too, so why did I stay? I didn't see myself as worthy for Allah to let me be the guest of the martyrs for a few days to learn lessons of self-sacrifice and loyalty from them. I looked towards the Kumayl Trench for the last time and I promised the martyrs I would return. I told them I would return to mention their memories to those that came after them.

We started to move with great difficulty. There was no more shooting or missiles. It was as if everything had paused so that these few people could return, perhaps so that the secret of the Kumayl Trench wouldn't be lost in the heart of the desert. After an hour, we reached the first trench. We could still see the Iraqi ambush trenches along the way, but they didn't believe any of the Iranian troops would still be alive. We continued moving through the night. Some of the soldiers were crawling, some dragging themselves along the ground. They had no strength left in their bodies. We then reached the Doqolu Mountains. After circling the mountains, we reached the Yasser Brigade stationed there. When they saw our faces, they came forward and asked, "Who are you? Where have you been?" We replied, "We are from the Kumayl Brigade." As soon as we reached our troops, I collapsed and fell unconscious, the others following suit. They quickly brought stretchers for us. The next day, I woke up in a military hospital in Chinaneh on a drip. Everybody who would come would ask where we had been, what we had been doing and where the others were.

Yes, we were to survive so that those who would come after us would know what kind of heroism Ibrahim Hadi and the other warriors displayed under siege.

THE SINCERE SERVANT OF ALLAH

In May 2009, we sent the book *'Peace be upon Ibrahim'* for a license after two years of research and preparation of the text during the days leading up to the martyrdom of Lady Fatimah (a). We really wanted Agha Ibrahim's book to be displayed at the programme for the martyred spies which coincided with the martyrdom of the Mother of the Imams, but the management told us that issuing a license takes a month. The next day, to our disbelief, they told us that the license to print the book was ready. Apparently, when the director read the book, he couldn't leave it for the next day and worked until the end of the day! Now we had to print the book, which was also very time-consuming, but we only had six days until the programme. I met the late Haj Aliyan, the former publications director of the magazine 'The Message of Freedom' and spoke to him about the printing. When he saw Ibrahim's photo, he recognised him and said, "I had seen him in Dokouheh." He then told me he would do whatever he could. I told him I had no money to print the book, but he replied, "That's no issue, but it's unlikely for five thousand copies of a book to be printed within a week as there is a book exhibition soon and all the printing centres are booked out." Later, when I would tell people the story, they couldn't believe it; my friends and I were busy boxing the books the night before Lady Fatimah (a)'s martyrdom! The book *'Peace be upon Ibrahim'* was printed and was displayed in the memorial for martyred spies.

From that day onwards, Ibrahim came back to life in this

material world. Many miracles have been witnessed all over this country from this sincere servant of Allah, miracles which testify to this martyr being present and living. Many of our friends advised us to add these to the book, but I replied, "These occurrences are nothing amazing. The whole of Ibrahim's life and martyrdom is a miracle as he was a true servant of Allah, and the Qur'an has told us that the martyrs are living." On the other hand, if we were to publish all the messages we had received about his miracles, they would be more than the first book, but some of these messages were so outstanding, they were even publicised on the media. In this section, we have given a few examples. Three years ago, a university student contacted us and said:

"I was a modern university student and indifferent towards religion. I was one of those students who bade farewell to their past and anything to do with religion after enrolling in university. For a while, my life went on like that until some of my friends said to me, "We want to go on Rahiyan-e Noor.[30] Come with us, you'll like it," so I went with them to have a good time. One night while I was on this journey, I felt sorry for myself while I was sitting with one of the narrators of the martyrs. I had ruined my past. That night, I dreamt that a war had broken out, a war like the wars of the beginning of Islam! I was wondering which army to join when I suddenly saw the Holy Prophet (s) organising his army. When he saw me, he ordered, "Go to Ibrahim's division." I thought the commander of the division was Prophet Ibrahim (a). I quickly joined Ibrahim's division. He was a luminous and handsome youth and when we got ready for battle, I woke up.

The next morning, I stayed away from my friends and started to reflect on my dream alone. The narrator of the caravan gathered the group and said, "I recommend that you read a book. I am sure that you won't get bored of reading it. I am sure that you will gain a lot from reading this book. It is a book by the name of

---

30 A traditional Iranian trip to the south of the country, normally to Fakkeh, to visit the battlefields

'*Peace be upon Ibrahim*'." He then picked the book up and showed it to the rest of the students. I had sat a little further away and was deep in thought when I heard him speaking. I looked at them from a distance. The face of the youth on the book was very familiar to me. I got up and walked to them. When I came closer, I recognised the photo. This youth was our commander, the same Ibrahim whom the Holy Prophet (s) had told me to join his division. I came forward and took the book from the narrator's hand, awestruck. It was him himself, I had no doubt. That day, I bought the book and went somewhere private so I could start reading it, but why had the Holy Prophet (s) told me to join Ibrahim's division? When I opened the first page of the book, I realised the book was dedicated to the Holy Prophet (s)! From that day onwards, Ibrahim has become my Muslim guardian and my brother in religion, and I am trying to stay firm and steadfast in Ibrahim's division."

After getting in contact often, he came to the Office of Publications and was telling us that he had a story for us. He said without an introduction:

"I had become quite old, but had a good job. I had gone for many marriage proposals, but each time, something would arise, and we wouldn't get married. One time, it was the issue of hijab, another time it was the issue of dowry and other times the issue of the difference of culture between the families. My mother and sister eventually became tired of searching. I was more distressed than anyone else. Days passed until two years ago, I went to Behesht-e Zahra on the 21st of April and we organised a little birthday party for Ibrahim next to his memorial. Many people came and listened to memories from Ibrahim's life. I was glad I was able to take a small step towards introducing him to the people. Once everybody left, I looked at Ibrahim's photo and said, "While you were alive, you would always struggle to resolve people's problems. Now you have been martyred and Allah says you are alive." I then said in my heart, "Ibrahim dear, everybody gives gifts for a birthday, but I am asking you for a gift. Do something so the next time I come to see you, I come with a wife!"

The next day, one of my friends called me and introduced a family to me [for marriage]. Even though I couldn't be bothered to do this again, I went with my mother and sister. All the stages went swimmingly, and I felt she was the one for me. There were no problems, not the dowry nor anything else. There were no disagreements between our families. After we finished speaking, they said to us, "Go to that room to talk about personal issues." As I entered the room with the girl, my eyes fell upon a large photo of Ibrahim on the wall! When I sat, my first question was, "Do you also know Shaheed Ibrahim Hadi?" She answered, surprised, "Yes, Shaheed Hadi was my father's comrade in the war. They lived in the same neighbourhood and I also believe in the great position of this martyr." In conclusion, I went to Behesht-e Zahra a week later. I went to his memorial with my wife and to thank him, we sat by him for an hour. I later found out my wife had also asked Ibrahim to find her a suitable husband.

THE MANNER OF INTRODUCTION

Narrator: One of the interviewees

I didn't have a good past and like many others, I wouldn't wear hijab and would wear makeup. I was indifferent towards religious issues and my life passed in futility and materialism, but I was always looking for a purpose, a way to find myself and understand how to live in this world until I was introduced to a teacher of one of the baseej classes.[31] I would attend her classes because I was

---

31 Classes which are normally held in mosques in Iran and they teach about values of the martyrs etc.

good friends with her. In one of her lessons, my new friend gave me the book *'Peace be upon Ibrahim'* to read and explain it in her class. I started to read the book on my own and however much time passed, I wasn't able to put the book down or stop thinking about the main character of the book. Ibrahim had a profound effect on my life. I could always see his handsome and innocent face in my mind. I was so enchanted by Shaheed Hadi's *akhlaq* and values that I would speak to this martyr in private. I often thought to myself, "Can the martyrs really hear our voices?"

The martyrs had also invited me because I attended these gatherings and the year after, we went to the warzones on the Rahiyan-e Noor trip. Even though I had been on many journeys both inside and outside the country, this trip was one of the best journeys of my life. One day during the trip, they took us to a place known as Me'raj-e Shuhada, the place where the bodies of the martyrs were kept. It was a very special place. I was constantly shouting out to Shaheed Hadi on the inside and was crying. I was thinking of him wherever I went, but I asked myself once again, "Does this mean that Shaheed Hadi can hear my voice?! Does he pay attention to me despite my past?" Unfortunately, that day in Me'raj-e Shuhada, I had put makeup on. I was deep in thought when a lady came next to me and kindly took my hand. She asked me without any kind of introduction, "Do you know Shaheed Ibrahim Hadi?" I said yes, startled. That lady told me, "My sister, Shaheed Hadi pays attention to you. Don't you know the martyrs pay a lot of attention to you now that you've turned to them? They wouldn't like you to sin." When she saw I was surprised, she gave me a white cloth she had in her hand and said, "This is from Shaheed Hadi. Wipe off your makeup!" She then added, "The martyrs are alive and can hear our voices." My eyes welled up with tears. I lowered my head and tears started to fall from my eyes. When I looked up again, I couldn't find that lady again! I sat right there in the Me'raj-e Shuhada building and started to weep. I then wiped off my makeup with the handkerchief and came out.

Only then did I realise the martyrs could hear our voices, they know what pains us and show us the path. I came to the conclusion that we must pay special attention to our actions like Shaheed Ibrahim. I made this martyr a role model for myself during my life and he truly took my hand. I advise the readers to build a friendship with this martyr as it is a two-way friendship. If you are with them, the martyrs will also be with you.

IBRAHIM, THE GUIDE

I left the department on Wednesday. I had a few books with me, and I was on my way home. We were given Thursday, Friday, and Saturday off for the Nights of Decree and the martyrdom of Imam Ali (a). It was a good opportunity for me to clarify the misconceptions I had about the Holy Defence. I got home and after a while, I looked at the books and chose one. There was nothing about a certain operation on the cover of the book. All the books I had chosen to research were long and all of them were about specific operations like Khaybar, Wal-Fajr 8 and Karbala 4. I thought to myself perhaps this book may also be about an operation. It was the smallest book and it would be easier for me to read. I laid down on my bed and started reading the book. This book was the memories from a martyr's life and had nothing to do with the operations, Shaheed Ibrahim Hadi. Whenever I would turn the page, my love for Ibrahim's personality would increase. I was so enchanted by his personality that I couldn't bring myself to put the book down.

That night, my aunt, her husband, and their children came to our house and like always, I opened the door without a scarf. I then sat down and continued reading the book. The more I read, I would recognise Ibrahim further and he would become dearer to me. I became so attached to him, I would become upset, cry and my heart would pain when I read he had been wounded. I would then think to myself, "Are you mad?! This book is about a martyr, which means he's not living anymore. Why are you getting so upset over his injuries?" When my family saw me crying at the end of the night, they asked, "Why are you crying so much?" I wiped my tears and answered, "Well, you don't know Ibrahim!" My aunt's husband explained to me, "The warfront was like that. I knew many people like Ibrahim. I understand why you're crying." That night ended with us speaking about the warfront, the war, and the martyrs.

The next morning, I started reading the book again, not to complete my research, but rather to know more about Ibrahim. I opened the book and reached the part where Ibrahim was scraping his eye with a needle and was reproaching himself for looking at *non-mahrams*. I closed the book. I didn't know what to do out of embarrassment! I started crying again, but this time, it was because I was so far from Ibrahim, and Allah! The book was finishing, but I felt I was starting again. I reached the stage of Ibrahim's martyrdom. I didn't want it to end. I didn't want to read about his end. When I read the name of Operation Before the Dawn, I thought to myself, "Oh my God!" I recognised the operation. When I researched Operation Wal-Fajr 8, I understood the alienation of the martyrs of Fakkeh. Ibrahim was one of the oppressed soldiers of the plains of Fakkeh who hurried towards Allah like a champion during this operation. When I finished the book, I wasn't myself anymore. It was as if I had lost my loved one. I started thinking deeply and reflecting on many things.

It was the Night of Decree. For many years, I had forgotten the rites of this night in my sleep of corruption. Like previous years, I went to bed and fell asleep. I couldn't believe it, but Ibrahim came in my dream! I saw Ibrahim. He came and said kindly, "Get up and pray, they're reciting the adhan!" I sat up and looked at him in my dream. He came closer and said, "You are the reputation of Islam!" I woke up. There were fifteen minutes left until the time of adhan. I started to cry uncontrollably and said, "O' Allah, am I the reputation of Islam? Me, the sinner?! I have ruined the reputation of Islam!" I went and performed Wudu.[32] In the morning after the Night of Decree, I prayed for the first time in years. Ibrahim had embarrassed me with his words. If I can't be the reputation of Islam, I should at least try not to ruin the reputation of Islam.

Today, I have chosen the chador of Lady Fatimah (a) as the best clothing for myself with Ibrahim's blessings. For this reason, I ask you that instead of behaving insolently with people who don't wear the hijab properly or don't understand our beliefs, let's be a guide like Ibrahim Hadi, and if we can't do so, we should introduce Ibrahim and people like him to them. Verily, Allah is All-Generous, All-Merciful. I try my best to compensate for the days I oppressed myself with disobedience to Allah and sins, and distanced myself from my God and beloved. I hope Allah will not take the blessing of worship away from me. Ibrahim gave me such a comfort that even if I forgot the whole world, I would still be comfortable. My heart wishes to tell you that Ibrahim not only changed me but even those around me. 'Peace of Allah be upon Ibrahim the day he was born, the day he was martyred and the day he shall be resurrected.' My dear friends, pray for me when you sit on your prayer mats as well so that Allah accepts my servitude. 2014, Ms SH S.

THE BROTHER'S INVITATION

Narrator: The martyr's sister

During these recent years, I have been blessed to be present in Fakkeh during the Iranian New Year and be the guest of the martyrs. I go so I can learn from great teachers as all we have is from the martyrs. I went to Fakkeh in the Iranian New Year 2015 and when we reached the trench, Ibrahim came just like when

---

32 The ritual ablutions consisting of washing the face, arms and wiping the head and feet which Muslims perform before praying or touching/reading the Qur'anic text

we were together! I started talking with him. We then entered the trench and they had prepared gift packs for the guests of the Kumayl Trench. Inside each pack, there was the name and details of a martyr, and each pack was different to the other. We got to know many martyrs like this. They told us to pay attention and see which martyr had invited us that year. They gave me a pack too and when I opened it, I was amazed to see Ibrahim's photo and details written on it. I felt ill and I sat down. Nobody there knew I was Ibrahim's sister. I said, "Thank you, Ibrahim, for inviting me this New Year's." On that piece of paper, there was a small message from Ibrahim which said, "Whatever you do must be only for Allah's pleasure."

On that journey, wherever I would go, Ibrahim would come with me. One night, we went to the campsite in Mishdagh. We hadn't contacted them in advance, nor did they recognise us. Normally under these circumstances, they wouldn't let us stay. I was worried we would have problems. The director of the campsite asked, "How many ladies are there?" and we told him there were thirty people. They said, "Please come inside. When you enter the hall, the second room is ready for you." As soon as I reached the second door, it said 'Shaheed Ibrahim Hadi Residence'. I said, "Thank you, my dear brother, for looking after your guests here as well." My friends asked me, "Did you book this room in advance?" I replied, "Believe me, I didn't!" That night, the ladies of our caravan told the volunteers at the campsite that Shaheed Hadi's sister was part of the caravan. Suddenly, I was surrounded by people who wanted me to talk to them about Ibrahim. They all knew Ibrahim and had read his book. When I finished talking, I said, "I've been attending classes of correct lifestyle and *akhlaq* for years, but none of them have been as effective for me as Ibrahim's *akhlaq*." On the Iranian New Year 2016, something similar happened. Once again, they gave me a present which had a piece of paper inside in the province of Fakkeh. They had put love letters to twenty different martyrs inside and I got Ibrahim's love letter!

After that journey, I was invited to Jamiatul Zahra[33] in Qom to speak to the foreign students about Ibrahim. There were three hundred students from different countries. When the meeting ended, sisters from countries like Germany, Italy, Egypt, Saudi Arabia, Yemen and Thailand came to me and each one would ask me questions with the book *'Peace be upon Ibrahim'* in their hands. I answered each of their questions. Just like the people of Iran, they considered Ibrahim a suitable role model for today's generation. They all said, "We shall convey the message of Ibrahim and your martyrs to our country." In these recent years, a member of one of the martyr's families created a website online in Ibrahim's name and they share photos and text about him. Interesting articles have been uploaded on the website and many people contacted us because of this. One of these articles which was more wonderful than the rest will be mentioned now. A young lady contacted us and told us she must tell us a story and Ibrahim had changed her view towards this world and the hereafter. Many people had contacted us like this and I thought that she had just changed like the other people who had read the book *'Peace be upon Ibrahim'* and had an inner revolution, but the changes witnessed in this lady were greater than we imagined. This young lady said:

"I am a Christian lady from the religious minorities of Tehran, and I didn't believe in the basis of *akhlaq* and not even the basis of religion. There was no corrupt action that I didn't do and every day, I would sink further into sin. Two, three years ago, some of my friends and I decided to go on holiday to a part of the country at New Year's, but we didn't know where to go; north, south, east or west. My friends said, "Let's go to Khuzestan. It has a beach and the weather is nice there." We went to Khuzestan in our own car from Tehran. We went to have a good time and we reached our destination one or two days later. We had a very good time on

---

33   A women's Islamic seminary in the holy city of Qom

the way. We got to the city at night and we couldn't find a hotel or a place to stay. One of our friends said, "We only have one choice; we have to go to the Rahiyan-e Noor campsites.' We all laughed as our appearances and faces weren't correct for such a place, but after driving around the city several times, we decided to wear our scarves, change our look and go to the Rahiyan-e Noor campsites. It took a little while for the management of Rahiyan-e Noor to accept us and they gave us a room. When we went in, the whole room was covered in photos of the martyrs. Each of my friends would mock the photos of the martyrs as a joke and would use bad language. A photo of a young man caught my eye and I joked with my friends, "This one is for me [to get married to]!" While we were leaving in the morning, I looked at the face of that youth again. Contrary to the others, the name of that martyr wasn't written and underneath the picture, only the following sentence was written, "I wish to remain unknown."

We had a good time and spent the rest of the journey in a hotel. A few days later, we went back to Tehran. A while later, I went to my university's library to find a book. While searching for a certain book, another book suddenly caught my attention. The youth on the cover was very familiar to me. It was him; the same youth whose photo I saw on the wall on my journey to Khuzestan. I remembered the jokes from that night. It was the same youth who wanted to remain unknown. I borrowed the book from the librarian. His name was Ibrahim Hadi and the name of his book was *'Peace be upon Ibrahim'*. I didn't like these kinds of people, but I started studying the book out of curiosity. I started to read the book and once I reached the middle of the book, I started to read out of love. Towards the end of the book, I didn't want his story to end and when I finished the book, it was as if a new path had been laid in front of me. I started to think in silence and in private. Ibrahim had overwhelmed my thoughts and my mind. This martyr had such a wonderful personality! That night, I wanted to choose

Ibrahim for myself as a joke, but apparently, he had chosen me! He made me eager to study the martyrs. His personality had a great impact on me. A while later, I started studying different religions and I researched Islam and the Ahlulbayt (ams) until Ibrahim became my Hadi[34] towards Islam. I became a Muslim. May Allah's peace be upon Ibrahim who familiarised me with Allah, Islam and the Ahlulbayt (ams).

THE GUEST
Narrator: Mrs Ali-Nejad

I first heard the Supreme Leader say the following sentence in 2010, "Keeping the memory of the martyrs alive is no less than martyrdom itself." I love the memories from the lives of the martyrs. One of the volunteers in the campsites of Rahiyan-e Noor told me about Shaheed Ibrahim Hadi's memories and his book. I searched a lot in my city Kahnuj but I couldn't find the book. I asked a few people where I could get the book from and they told me, "They have this book in Rafsanjan." I called their office in Rafsanjan, but they informed me their books were sold out. I told them, "I am the director of Jamiatul Qur'an[35] in Kahnuj. I want to introduce a few sisters who are learning and are hafid[36] of the Qur'an to this martyr." They gave me a number for their office in Tehran but after following up several times and not hearing anything back, I asked Imam Mahdi (aj) for his help and asked him to send this martyr to me to guide me if he saw fit. I then called Tehran again and all thanks to Allah, they said they had it. I set up a book-reading competition for Daheh-ye Fajr.[37] I paid the money for

---

34   In Arabic, the word Hadi means guide

35   A school where women can go and learn how to read and memorise the Qur'an

36   Hafid of the Qur'an means somebody who has memorised the complete Qur'an

37   The ten days between the arrival of Imam Khomeini (ra) to Iran and the success of the Islamic Revolution of Iran (1st of February-11th of February)

the books and they confirmed the books had been sent. They also sent some other books about other martyrs which were published by the Shaheed Hadi Group. I was waiting eagerly. I still hadn't seen this martyr's face and also, I was eager to read his book.

Early in the morning, I turned onto the street of Jamiatul Qur'an and I saw the receptionist washing the road with a hose and had also spread roses all over the road like when the Imam (ra) returned to Iran! I said angrily, "Sister, Kahnuj has a water shortage. What are you doing? Why are there roses here? What's happening?" The receptionist came and said joyfully, "Don't you know? We have guests, and they are such good guests!" When she saw I was surprised, she continued, "Today, the martyrs are our guests and they are coming to the institute now!" I ran into the street to see what was going on and suddenly, I saw a group of handsome and radiant youths walking down the road. They had beautiful coats and trousers on, and they were speaking and laughing with one other. There was a large crowd behind them as well. There was one person amongst the martyrs whose face was overly radiant, and everyone was standing next to him. I ran into the institute to tell the ladies to wear their chadors as the martyrs were about to arrive. When I went into the institute, I could smell perfume and wild rue everywhere. There was a woman waiting at the door with a Qur'an in her hand. It was as if the students knew that the martyrs were coming before me. Inside the institute, I looked at the doors and walls with amazement. Where was this place?! It was as if Jamiatul Qur'an in Kahnuj had become a palace! Such beautiful carpets, such beautiful curtains, and there was a wonderful light emerging from it, emitting the smell of roses.

While I was appreciating these scenes, I suddenly woke up. It was Friday morning, and it was a very blessed one. I cried my heart out. I was overjoyed that the martyrs came to the institute. I didn't utter a word about this dream to a single soul. The books were scheduled to arrive that day and had to be distributed, but I was worried in case it was late and didn't arrive in time for the competition. That afternoon, we got a call from the terminal and they told us several boxes of books had arrived. I went to the offices with my husband and we picked up several large boxes. When we reached the door of the institute, my husband picked up the first box, but it was heavy and it slipped from his hands onto the floor. The box ripped and the books fell out in front of me. I was staring at the books. The photo on the cover of the book lying in front of me was of the same youth who was standing in the middle of the group of martyrs last night, and the other books had the other martyrs on them. I felt my knees weaken and I sat on the floor. My eyes had welled up with tears. I picked up the martyrs' books respectfully and welcomed them each one by one. These were the same youths who were our guests at the institute the night before. I remembered their faces well. The person in the middle was Ibrahim Hadi and the people to his side were Shaheed Alamdar and Shaheed Towraji. My husband, who didn't know about my dream, said, "What are you doing? Come and help me pick up the books." It was a strange Friday night. The martyrs had arrived!

Allah is my witness that since we hosted the martyrs in Jamiatul Qur'an, our conditions have completely changed and improved day by day. The doors of virtue and blessing have been opened upon us. We had started our work with great difficulty in this deprived province of the country and now, by the blessing of the martyrs, we have been endowed with such an honour. I thought of Ibrahim like a brother. My first request for Ibrahim was for him to ask Allah to give me the modesty of Lady Fatimah (a), a modesty so that I can stay away from *non-mahrams*, not look at *non-mahrams* and also, so that *non-mahrams* do not see me, as the Mother of our Masters said, "The best state which draws a woman closer to her

Lord is that she shouldn't interact with the *non-mahrams* [as much as she can]." I then asked him to make me a sincere servant of Allah. From that day onwards, Agha Ibrahim has been resolving my problems, problems for which I should have got help from the Imam of the Friday prayers or the court. It was necessary for me to go in person and speak to resolve these issues. Before I left, I said to Ibrahim very informally, "Are you okay with me speaking to *non-mahrams*? You resolve the problem yourself and sort everything out. I will send a letter, you can follow up." Believing such a thing is not difficult for those who have faith. My problems would be resolved without me following up the letter at all!

I remembered on the first day, I asked my master to send me this martyr to guide us, and what a great teacher Imam Mahdi (aj) sent to guide us! Days passed and our activities broadened. One Thursday night, I recited Ziyarah Ashura on behalf of Imam Mahdi (aj), his young mother and the martyrs, and I said, "Dash Ibrahim, the teachers of this institute struggle sincerely and humbly in this city which is crying out for cultural activities. I am very embarrassed. Please ask Allah to give me the blessing to take the teachers to Karbala on the 15th of Sha'ban." If you think about it materialistically, when you take the cost of such a trip into account, it is impossible to do so, but he replied to me very quickly. On the 15th of Sha'ban, I was sitting in Bayn al-Haramayn[38] with ten of the other Qur'an teachers and we did *ziyarah* on behalf of the martyrs. What a great journey it was, a journey organised by the martyrs. Yes, ever since the martyrs were our guests, our lives have changed, and even the city has changed. The words of Allah reverberate around the city. Ibrahim, this great man of sincerity and action, was a lantern in our city for all those who wished to be a servant in Allah's court. Ibrahim came to our long-lost city to guide us to the path. Now, many of the people of our city know him, and we can write a book about the miracles which have taken

---

38   The area between Imam Husayn (a)'s and Hazrat Abbas (a)'s shrines

place here themselves. The story of Reza is one of these miracles.

REZA

Narrator: A message from one of the sisters from Jamiatul Qur'an in Kahnuj

Our story began fifteen years ago when I was pregnant. Towards the end of my pregnancy, I was very ill and in the eighth month of my pregnancy, the doctor told me that the baby had died in my womb! I was shocked and I cried a lot. I went to some other doctors and they said, "There is a minute chance that your child is still alive, but under these circumstances, we must carry out a C-section immediately." That night, I sook intercession from Imam Rida (a) and cried out to him, "I ask you for my child. If it is a boy and he is healthy, I will name him Reza." They carried out the surgery and unbelievably, my son arrived in this world alive, but he weighed only nine-hundred grams! Our son was raised with great difficulty and required a lot of care. He learnt to speak late at the age of three. My son grew up, but he had physical weakness, and this condition continued until after he finished primary school. As the nearest high school was relatively far, my husband was opposed to the idea of sending him to school and said, "Our son has an illness and can't walk that far."

The academic year began and our Reza stayed at home. I was very upset for him and he was also becoming increasingly frustrated; I didn't know what to do. In those days, I would attend classes at Jamiatul Qur'an in Kahnuj. One day, the director spoke to us about the martyrs, gave us a book a martyr and said, "Definitely read this book. We have a book-reading competition for Daheh-ye Fajr." The name of the book was *'Peace be upon Ibrahim'*. That night, I started reading the book and I cried a lot when I read some of the memories from this martyr's life. At midnight, I closed the book and put it under my pillow. I started to tell this martyr my problems until I fell asleep. As soon as I fell asleep, I sensed that my bedroom door opened. Shaheed Ibrahim Hadi came in with a cup in his hand. I stared at him with amazement. The martyr came forward and put the cup in front of me. There were several pieces of paper inside the cup, like a ballot. I took one of the pieces of paper and on it was written, "Seek intercession for him." I exclaimed, "Should I ask intercession for him? From whom? From where?" Ibrahim Hadi said, "From the same person who brought your nine-hundred-gram child here; from Imam Rida (a)." I jumped from my sleep and I thought to myself, "How should I seek intercession for my son? How can I take Reza to Mashhad?" Our family's financial status wasn't good. I said, "O' Allah, with what money should I take Reza to Mashhad?" but I thought to myself, "Allah can do anything. He will definitely help us."

The next morning, I went to Jamiatul Qur'an and I told my dream to the director of the institute. She said, "Insha'Allah, it's good. Definitely go to Mashhad." I answered sorrowfully, "We don't have much money. Also, I've taken this child to Mashhad several times before, but he hasn't changed." The director of the institute responded, "If Allah wills, your journey will be organised. This time you go to Mashhad, tell Imam Rida (a) that Ibrahim Hadi has sent you. Whatever you want from this kind Imam, he will give to you." The next day, they informed us that the Propagation Department is taking a few members of religious organisations to Mashhad. I put my name down too and a few days later, my name was somehow drawn from the ballot! A week later, to my disbelief, I was in the shrine of Imam Rida (a) with my son Reza who had a problem walking. Looking at his shrine, I invoked the Imam (a), "I have brought Reza to you. I have been sent by Shaheed Ibrahim Hadi, so do whatever you see fit." By the blessings of Allah and Imam Rida (a), after our journey to Mashhad, my son's health became better day by day. He went to high school and continued his lessons, and now, he is successful in his life.

TO ALLAH

Narrator: Mrs Khorrami

(an interview from the programme Lak Jeegh on the Iranian channel 2)

I was born in 1980, but I was reborn four years ago. I was one of those women who had no aspect of spirituality in their lives, and I was always searching for something materialistic to feel content. My financial situation was good and I would get whatever I wanted. I searched everywhere, in sport, work, friends and acquaintances, but I didn't achieve true contentment. I was a very successful athlete and was even picked for the national team, but I still wasn't content. I really hated women who wore the hijab. Whenever I was behind the steering wheel and I saw a woman driving in a chador, I would remark snidely, "Either protect your chador or drive." I didn't see any use for the chador. I believed the chador was opposed to the freedom and progress of women. My daughter, who was in high school, had exactly the same mindset and behaviour as myself. Those days, the only good thing I would do was that I would go to Kahrizak and help the poor people who lived there. Once, I calculated I must have a lot of good deeds as I would go there once a week and would do so for a few years.

Once, I went to one of my friends who used to take faal[39] from Hafez's poems. I made the intention to know what Allah thought of me. When my friend took the faal for me, she said to me, "Do you think you have anything on Allah?! Do you want Allah to expose you and say what you have done?!" I didn't understand what this faal meant. To that day, I had done many good things for Allah's sake. When she said this, my eyes welled up with tears and I started crying. Believe me, I went home and cried for three whole days. I went back to the same friend afterwards and she immediately said to me, "Come towards spirituality and redeem your past." I thought to myself, "I can't, I've created a special routine for myself that isn't

---

39   Something similar to an *istikharah*, but taken from the poems of a poet by the name of Hafez, who was a God-fearing person

compatible with spirituality. Every morning when I wake up, I put on makeup first and wear a different set of clothes," but after a few days of contemplation, I decided to at least start praying. I thought to myself that the first step is to give importance to fasting and prayer, but not hijab. A short while later, I bought myself a long and wide manto[40] and I tried to keep my hair inside my scarf. These things were relatively easy, but removing makeup from my life was impossible. I reflected, "Now that I've taken the first step, I should go all the way." When I thought about it, I realised that this style of life was more love-centred as my life revolved around Allah. I slowly removed makeup from my life, but it did take a while. The next issue was socialising with *non-mahrams*. In every gathering, I would shake hands with *non-mahrams*. I asked Allah to resolve this problem for me and I kept traveling on this path with Allah's help. The next year, I decided to wear the chador. It may have been difficult, but I had to start sometime. One day after dropping my son off at the gym, I went to the shop with a friend and bought a chador. I started to wear the chador in that very shop and I have never looked back. You can't imagine how much comfort it brought to me. Sometimes, I would think to myself, "You used to mock those who wear chadors a lot, but now look at yourself!" After a short while, I registered for baseej classes in my neighbourhood.

    The path of my life had completely changed, but my daughter was still on the wrong path. I had trained her to live the same way I used to before and now that I had chosen a new way of life, she distanced herself from my actions and she didn't accept my lifestyle at all. When I saw I couldn't change her, I told her, "You must be in love to change. I won't force you, but I know that one day, you will fall in love with Allah and will become like me." My daughter would laugh at me and say, "Never!" Even when she would come to see me at the baseej base, she would purposefully expose her hair and put on more makeup than usual. A while

---

40   A long dress that Muslim women wear to cover their bodies

later, my daughter's high school announced they wanted to take the students to Rahiyan-e Noor. My daughter took permission and went on the trip to have a good time with her friends. When she was leaving, I said to her, "Insha'Allah when you return, you'll start praying again," but my daughter laughed in my face again and said, "Never!" Every night, my daughter would call me from Rahiyan-e Noor and say, "They tell us that the martyrs have invited us here," and then she would laugh, mock them and say, "I don't believe that one bit!" However, day by day, I sensed that the spirituality of the military regions was slowly influencing her.

One time during those days, I went to the mosque to attend a programme. I don't know why I was restless that day! I sat in several different places and the last place I sat in, I saw a piece of paper had fallen next to me. I picked the paper up and started to read it. It was the biography of a martyr. I felt as if Allah wanted me to get to know this martyr. I took the piece of paper, took permission from the director of the baseej classes at that mosque and took it with me. I read it with a lot of excitement. That piece of paper was a short biography of a sincere martyred athlete by the name of Ibrahim Hadi. That day, I spoke with the photo of the martyr and asked him to help my daughter. I said, "I am sure that you can guide my daughter to spirituality." That night, my daughter called me again and said, "Mum, the narrator of our caravan always tells us memories from the life of a martyr which were very beautiful, a martyr by the name of Ibrahim Hadi. Will you let me buy the book of this martyr's memories?" I remembered the leaflet I found that day and said excitedly, "Definitely buy it!" I was sure that was it. From what had happened that day, I was sure that Ibrahim would become the Hadi of my daughter.

From here, I will narrate from my daughter:

"There was a strange atmosphere in Rahiyan-e Noor. The whole place was a desert, but you can't imagine what kind of strange atmosphere there was. I took a portion of the dust from there with me. However, the most important thing that happened on this trip was getting to know Ibrahim. The book *'Peace be upon Ibrahim'* had a great effect on me. I had read many books, but this book was truly wonderful. When I returned, I read the book and it had a great effect on me. I decided to pray, but I delayed it because I was too stubborn to pray in front of my mother. I had secretly started to pray, but it slowly became open. I was an athlete and I would play volleyball. Ibrahim was also an athlete, a champion of wrestling and volleyball. I always talk to him and whenever I go to a competition or an exam, I ask him to help me. I make oaths with Ibrahim, pray for him and I always see Allah's blessing in all my problems. A while later, I started to wear the chador and I became like my mother. My friends ask many questions about the changes in myself."

In my own words, I say, "I had tried everything. I had money and everything [I wanted] at my disposal, every kind of comfort, but Allah's path is very pleasant, and all it requires is love. The chador has rules to observe and when you know these rules, you will fall in love with it. At first, I thought it would be difficult, but after protecting my hijab for a month, I was inseparable from the chador. The chador is like a fort which protects the woman. My life has changed completely. I now take more enjoyment from my current life than my previous life."

THE CHILD'S CURE

Narrator: Mortaza Parsaeiyan

Years after the era of Holy Defence, I was working as a blacksmith in a religious centre in 2014. I had ordered some iron. The driver of the Nissan came and asked, "Where should I put the delivery?" After delivering the package, he came to me to get his money. When he came into my office, he took a cup to take water from

the water dispenser. His eyes fell upon the photo of Agha Ibrahim on the wall. He stared at the photo, the cup in his hand, and said, "May Allah have mercy on you, Agha Ibrahim!" I was looking at the receipt, but I looked up and asked with surprise, "Were you on the warfront with Agha Ibrahim?" He said no though. "Did you live in the same neighbourhood as him?" I asked. However, he said no again. "So how do you know him?" I asked. He let out a deep sigh and said, "It's a long and unbelievable story. Leave it!" I owe my whole life to Ibrahim, so I went closer and said, "I'm intrigued, tell me what happened."

When the driver noticed my eagerness, he said; "I live in Varamin. I have had a truck for fifteen years and I do deliveries. I was delivering a package to 17 Shahrivar Street in Tehran. I went to the house. My young daughter was playing with a few other children outside the house. I went into the room and started to talk. A few minutes later while I was speaking, I suddenly heard the neighbour scream. I ran out the house and I saw my daughter had fallen into the farming pool on the land adjacent to the house. She had fallen into the water and before the adults knew, she had already swallowed some of the dirty water. My wife ran to put her chador on and we rushed our daughter to the hospital. Our daughter was in a very bad state. The doctor at the accident and emergency examined her and they took x-rays of her lungs. A few minutes later, the doctor called me over and said, "We'll do what we can, but the polluted water has entered this girl's lungs and it's unlikely this problem will be resolved." I was extremely upset. My wife was sitting beside my daughter's bed, but she didn't know what had happened. I didn't say anything either and comforted her. The customer's delivery was still in the truck, so I said to my wife, "I'm going to deliver the package. Just pray." I left, but I didn't have much hope. I made the delivery to 17 Shahrivar Street, close to the bridge over the Mohallati Highway. While I was unloading the truck, my eyes fell upon the face of a martyr drawn on the wall. He had an alluring and heavenly face. I went closer and looked at his face, then I said, "I am sure you are one of those drawn close to Allah. I am sure you have a position close to Allah. I am asking you to pray for my daughter and ask Allah to return her to us." I said this and went back to the hospital. I read the name of the martyr written below the photo; Shaheed Ibrahim Hadi.

That night, I was in the hospital with my wife. It was a difficult night and all the doctors had lost hope. I was in the prayer room, hoping for some relief regarding my daughter's situation. In the early morning, I fell asleep momentarily and I saw a handsome youth entered, pointed to me, and said, "Your daughter has been cured. Go to your daughter." He said this and left. I jumped from my sleep and ran towards the ICU. There was a great clamour; my daughter had regained consciousness! She was crying and the nurses were with her. The chief consultant of the unit also came. They took new x-rays of her lungs and the doctors said that the water had been absorbed by her body and it had gone, but I knew what had happened. The youth I saw in my dream was Ibrahim Hadi, except his face was brighter and he was wearing Kurdish trousers."

When he said this, I asked, "What is your daughter doing now?" He replied, "She is studying engineering in university now. Our whole house is full of photos of this martyr. We love him very much. Our daughter bought his book and we've read it several times." I remarked, looking at him with wonder, "It's very difficult to believe this. Do you agree?" The driver said, "Coincidentally, I have kept the x-rays of my daughter's lungs for fifteen years. The first photo shows her lungs full of water and the next shows no trace of water in the lungs."

THE CROWN OF SERVITUDE

Narrator: Text messages and e-mails

When Ibrahim was amongst the inhabitants of this world, he would often advise his sisters and relatives about their hijab. All those close to him were very attentive to observing the hijab correctly. Ibrahim would say to his sisters, "The chador is a souvenir of Lady Zahra (a). A woman's faith is complete once she observes the hijab to perfection. If you wish for your role model to be Lady Zahra (a), you must act in a way for her to be pleased with you." Ibrahim's still pays great attention to the hijab and this can be understood from the messages we have received. In most of the advice Ibrahim had given to his sisters in religion, he emphasised heavily on the crown of servitude: the hijab. The following stories are from these messages and e-mails:

Salaam to all of Shaheed Ibrahim Hadi's friends and lovers,

I got to know this great martyr by chance when I saw photos and articles of Shaheed Hadi online. At first, I hated religious people and for this reason, looking at his photo was so disgustful to me that I scrolled past the articles and photos without reading them. All I understood from it was that the book *'Peace be upon Ibrahim'* introduced this champion martyr. By chance, my husband bought this book for me and praised him. One day when I was bored, I started to read the book, but I hated looking at the cover! It was written in such a way that one wouldn't get bored reading it and I wanted to see what would happen at the end. I read the book and then I read it a few more times, laughing and crying at the stories. Each time I read it, I would understand what kind of a positive and exemplary personality he had better than before. I had recognised Dash Ibrahim to a certain extent, and I recommended the book to all my friends.

One day, I went to Behesht-e Zahra. (Of course, I must say in brackets that at that time, I wasn't observing hijab properly and

I didn't believe in anything. Even when I read the book and saw that Ibrahim emphasised heavily on the issue of hijab, I still went without hijab!) Anyway, I went in that same state to the cemetery of the martyrs. I searched the whole Sector 26 and I swear by the martyr himself, there was no trace of Shaheed Hadi! I searched the whole sector several times but I didn't find it. I looked at the placard and it said I was in Sector 26! I asked a soldier and he told me that there was no Shaheed Hadi there! After an hour of searching, I wasn't able to do *ziyarah* of Shaheed Hadi. On my way home, I felt upset and started crying. I felt the martyr didn't want to see me. A few months passed and many things happened in my life. I made my final decision and I reached Allah! I started to wear the hijab and pray. The first time I wore the chador, I went to Behesht-e Zahra. I said I would promise Shaheed Hadi I would observe the hijab the way he likes. I take Allah as my witness, when I reached Sector 26, I parked my car in the same place as the last time I visited. I saw a large photo of Shaheed Hadi above his memorial right in front of me! Only Allah knows how I felt. The last time I had come here, I had searched the whole sector grave by grave, but I didn't find the commander of my heart, but now...! I don't think Shaheed Hadi wanted to see me in that state.

This was the start of Ibrahim's revolution within me. From then on, my dear Shaheed Hadi has been very kind to me, he has helped me a lot and has made me indebted to him. I propagate his name and virtues everywhere I go, and I am proud that Shaheed Hadi brought me to Allah. A short while later, I was invited to the place which was a pathway to heaven, where the purest youths ultimately met their Lord; I visited the Kumayl Trench. Insha'Allah, the commander of our hearts, Agha Ibrahim Hadi, will take all our hands.

I didn't understand what the hijab was. I believed that only our beliefs counted and I gave no [religious] importance to my appearance. No one from our family wore the hijab, but our foundations were deeply rooted in religion. Sometimes, we would go to religious gatherings, but of course, we would go in bad hijab. I lived like this for eighteen years. I loved sport and enjoying myself, but I would pray at any cost. I was an attention seeker. I wanted everyone to notice me and to be the best. I thought that if people noticed me, my status would increase. I only had one friend who wore the chador and once, she spoke to me about the martyrs. Her words intrigued me. My friend bought me a book of memories from a martyr's life. I had read many books and novels, but I had never read a book about a martyr. I read the book. It was called *'Peace be upon Ibrahim'*. He had a very attractive personality and I didn't want the book to end. I felt as if the martyr was alive and his book hadn't come to me for no reason. One of the stories which had a great effect on me was when he didn't care if others noticed him. When he realised that a few girls had fallen for him, he even changed the way he dressed so that he wouldn't attract any more attention, but look at me! Many times, I had put several photos of myself on social media and I would become happy when many boys and girls would write comments underneath the photo!

For a while, my mind was engaged with Shaheed Ibrahim Hadi. My best friend told me several times to think about prayers, Allah, and the hijab, and then to make the correct decision. Many thoughts flew through my mind. If I was to wear the hijab, what would I say to my friends and family?! I reached the conclusion that I had experienced everything and have had all kinds of friends, but I had seen no good in them, so I thought to myself, "Let me go towards the hijab for the sake of Allah. Let me abandon whatever I like about my appearance in the way of Allah." During the days leading to Lady Fatimah (a)'s martyrdom last year, my family wanted to go to Behesht-e Zahra. I went with them on the condition we could find Ibrahim Hadi's memorial and visit him. When I found his memorial, I asked him to help me. I said, "I want to visit your memorial next time with hijab on, but I am a little bit scared." The next time I went to Behesht-e Zahra was two months later, and this time I went to his memorial with hijab on. I thanked Allah that he sent me such a good guide.

I had a very bad problem in my life and it wasn't resolved whatever I did. My intercession and duas were all inconclusive. I would pray, but I didn't believe in the concept of the hijab. I would supplicate a lot during my prayers, but I couldn't understand why it didn't work. For days, my problem was still at hand until I saw a youth in my dream who promised he would resolve my problems. I was overjoyed and asked his name, but he replied, "I am the unknown." I said, "Everyone has a name," but he replied again, "Call me the unknown." A few days later, the great problem in my life was miraculously resolved. I was ecstatic, and I was sure that it was resolved by divine help and the prayers of that unknown youth who I saw in my dream. I didn't know who that youth was. He had a luminous face, but I didn't know whether he was alive or dead, human or angel.

A few days later, I saw that great and unknown person in my dream again. I immediately thanked him and I was waiting to see what he would say. After a few moments of quiet, he said, "Now that your problem has been resolved, try and promise me that you will observe your hijab better than before." I promised him and woke up. From then on, the chador became my best friend as I had promised that unknown youth. I also researched the concept of hijab in detail and tried to observe my hijab well. A few days later, I was looking for an article online and suddenly, I saw a picture whose face was very familiar to me. I quickly clicked on the photo and opened the page. The photo was of the same youth who introduced himself as unknown to me! You can't imagine how glad I was. I started to search for information regarding him with a strange enthusiasm and I read his name, written as, "The unknown martyr, Ibrahim Hadi." I had finally recognised him and found a lot of information about him online. I am so joyful. I had spent years hating the hijab and the chador, but now, I have been wearing the hijab of Lady Fatimah (a) for more than a year, and I thank Allah for all His blessings.

And there are many stories of this ilk...

SHORT MEMORIES FROM THE LIFE OF A GREAT PERSON

Barefoot

He had come to the Office of Publications to buy books and was saying, "We have a religious gathering today and I intend to give the people spiritual food as well as dinner." He bought a few copies of *'Peace be upon Ibrahim'*. He picked up one of the books and looked at Shaheed Hadi's face with regret. He smiled bitterly and said to himself, "Look at where humans can reach!" I looked at him amazed and asked, "Did you know Agha Ibrahim? Do you remember a memory from his life?" He started thinking and a few minutes later, he said, "I used to live on Zeeba Street before the Revolution. Well, almost everyone in the neighbourhood knew Ibrahim. A good trait Ibrahim had was that he would help everybody. The world held no value in his eyes. If you would say, "Agha Ibrahim, your shirt is so nice," believe me, if he had anything on underneath the shirt, he would take it off then and there and give it to you.

One summer afternoon, I was sitting in the street, bored. It was very hot. I saw there was no point in wasting my time, I might as well go home and sit in front of the cooler. As I was leaving, I saw Ibrahim coming from the end of Zeeba Street which is now called Shaheed Mahdi Mashhadi Rahimi Street. I waited to meet Ibrahim and then leave. When he came closer, I noticed that he was barefoot. In this hot weather, his feet were burning so he would walk quickly. He was trying to walk in the shade while I was looking at him with surprise. I assumed he had been at the mosque and someone had taken his shoes. When he arrived, I said salaam and shook his hand. He quickly came into the shade. I pointed at his feet and asked, "Where are your shoes, why are you barefoot in this boiling weather?! Wait, let me bring you some slippers, have they taken your shoes at the mosque?" He replied, "No, I gave them away myself." I asked with surprise, "To whom?! Does a normal human being give his shoes as a gift in this weather and walk barefoot?" I questioned him to the extent that he was forced to speak, but he wouldn't normally say these things to people. Ibrahim looked at my face and said, "An old man was begging outside of the mosque and he was very poor. The old man pointed to the heels of his shoes which were worn out and he didn't have anything to wear. He was saying that his feet were burning in the heat, so I gave him my shoes because I had no money." He said goodbye before I could bring him slippers and left.

The Tin Can

It was two o'clock in the morning on Thursday night and we were working at a checkpoint in front of Mohammadi Mosque (close to the Shaheed Mohallati Highway). A few other youths and I were sitting on the steps of the mosque with Ibrahim Hadi and he was speaking with us. Suddenly, he got up and ran towards the road opposite us which was approximately a hundred metres away! He crouched down, put his hand in the gutter and came back. I asked, "Agha Ibrahim, what happened?" He replied, "Nothing, a tin can had fallen into the gutter and as it was floating past, it was making a lot of noise. I went and took it out of the water so that its noise wouldn't disturb those who were sleeping." He would teach us, teenagers, how to live properly through his actions.

The Bed

It was just like previous nights. When I woke up at midnight, I saw Ibrahim sleeping on the floor again. Even though we had laid out a bed for him, when he came from the mosque at midnight, he slept on the carpet again. I called him and said, "My dear brother, it's cold outside, you'll freeze. Why don't you sleep in your bed?" He replied, "It's fine, there's no need." When I insisted several times, he finally explained, "My friends on the warfront in Gilan-e Gharb are suffering from the cold and difficulties. I should also experience what they're going through."

Wrestling

We had gone to the Gym Championships and Ibrahim was sitting next to me amongst the audience. His most important opponent was someone called Qolipour. He had a strong body and would easily defeat his opponents. His friends encouraged him from the audience. He then sat among the audience to take a rest. Agha Qolipour turned to us and asked, "My next opponent is Ibrahim Hadi, do you know him?" Before I could say anything, Ibrahim said, "I know him. He's not that strong, you'll defeat him easily!" Qolipour went to the dressing room, happier than before, and started to warm up. A few minutes later, the chairman called Ibrahim and Qolipour's names for the next fight. Ibrahim was sitting in his place when they called his name for the second time. Qolipour and the referee were already in the arena. Ibrahim took off his clothes as he had his wrestling uniform on underneath and went to the arena. The referee checked Ibrahim's body and blew the whistle. Qolipour, who had readied himself for the fight, looked at Ibrahim and exclaimed, "But you..." Before he could finish his sentence, Ibrahim picked him up, spun him around and threw him down. Moments later, they announced that Qolipour had been knocked out. Ibrahim immediately helped him stand, kissed him and apologised to him. He then said, "I'm sorry. I am your friend. Forgive me." No one could believe this fight could be the foundation to their friendship. They became good friends and had a good relationship until Ibrahim's martyrdom.

The Religious Gathering

Whenever Ibrahim would come to the religious gatherings with his friends, there would be a special passion in the gathering. He would do all he could in beating his chest and reciting for the Ahlulbayt (ams), but he had specific habits in the religious gatherings. He wouldn't shout while reciting and he wouldn't allow them to increase the volume of the microphone. Before the religious gathering would begin, he would turn the speakers towards the hall so the neighbours wouldn't be bothered. He wouldn't allow the youths who had more of a passion to continue their mourning in the public gathering longer than usual. He was careful people wouldn't be bothered by the majlis of the Ahlulbayt (ams). He would pay special attention to these issues. Also, he would leave the gathering before they switched the lights back on. I only learnt why he would do so after. I saw the youths joking and laughing after the majlis and this would lower the spirituality they had gained from the majlis.

The Teacher

During the war, we had a teacher who had a great effect on me and my classmates. Many of his students started to pray and went to the warfront. One day, I said to him, "Thank Allah you are our teacher." Our teacher replied, "Make your prayers for Shaheed Ibrahim Hadi. He brought me here!" He then continued, "I was friends with Asghar Vesali, but I was rejected to study education at the beginning of the Revolution. I saw Ibrahim at Shaheed Vesali's funeral. I was happy to see him and I said salaam to him. Ibrahim, who knew me to an extent, replied to my salaam and asked, "What are you doing now?" I replied, "I failed the difficult teaching exams!" From the morning the next day, Ibrahim started to follow up on my work. He used to work alongside the Education and Nurturing Department, but because of their excessive strictness towards the beginning of the Revolution, he separated from them. In conclusion, I am only a teacher because of this great martyr's efforts."

The Desk

At the beginning of the Revolution, Ibrahim was working with the revolutionary committee. The committee's activities were very widespread, and people would mostly refer to the committees if they had a problem. I went to the committee where Ibrahim was working. There were a few rooms next to each other and in each room, there was a desk and one of the employees would sit behind the desk to respond to people's queries. I went to Ibrahim's room and contrary to the other rooms, the desk was behind him and the chair was in front of the desk. The people's chairs were also closer to his chair. I asked him what the difference was between this room and the other rooms, and he replied, "When I sat behind the desk, I felt a sense of pride. I felt distanced from the people in this way and for that reason, I brought the chair on this side so that the people could be closer to me."

Food

Mahdi Hasan Qummi, one of Ibrahim's youngest friends, relates:

Ibrahim would train us indirectly. For example, whenever we were together and we would come across a poor person, he would give me money to give to him. In this way, he wouldn't show off and he would also teach us how to behave with the poor. I remember

Ibrahim liked to eat Olivier salad sandwiches, but he wouldn't eat sandwiches from everywhere. There was a sandwich shop on 17 Shahrivar Street whose owner was known as Agha Sheikh as he was a holy and religious person. Ibrahim would always go to him and had a tab with him. He knew that he didn't put processed meats in his Olivier salad and would only use chicken. Ibrahim never ate processed sausages, hamburgers, or anything like that. In this manner, he taught us not to eat from anywhere and not to buy food from everywhere. He knew that this shopkeeper paid special attention to halal and haram food and he would go there for that very reason as the Qur'an orders, "A person must pay attention to the food he eats."

Kindness

Ibrahim's kind heart was the greatest blessing Allah bestowed upon him. One day while he was wounded, I went to visit him and one of the scholars was also there. Ibrahim was telling his memories from the warfront and said, "During one of the operations, I had gone towards the enemy at midnight and managed to get quite close to them by hiding amongst the trees and bushes. There was an Iraqi soldier in front of me and suddenly, I jumped out in front of him. There was no one else around. I curled my hand into a fist and thought to myself, 'I'll kill him with a punch," but when I stood in front of him, I felt sorry for him. He had his weapon slung on his shoulder and wasn't expecting anyone to come this close to him. He had such an innocent face, I felt sorry for him. He was a soldier who had been forced to go to war. Instead of hitting him, I hugged him and felt his body shiver like a leaf. I held his hand and brought him back. I then handed him over to one of my friends to send him back to the base and I went forward to continue the operation."

The Role Model

Our friendship with the youth in that day and age was based on laughing, playing, and bothering others. For example, a few guys would meet up, take the helmet of one of the workers who was passing by, throw it around and bother others, but friendship with Ibrahim meant taking him as a role model and learning morals. He would indirectly teach us the correct way to live and would even say things which we only would understand the depth of years after.

I had nice hair. I would always comb it and have different hairstyles. Many people were jealous of my hair and appearance. Ibrahim was also very handsome. One time when we were sitting together, they started to talk about my hairstyles again, but Ibrahim said a sentence which I will never forget, "Don't rub the blessings Allah has given to you into others' faces." Ibrahim said this and left.

Reputation

I was on my way home from school and I saw my friends Sayyid Kamal and (Shaheed) Naser Kermani sitting at the end of the road, so I went to join them. In that day, the youth would entertain themselves by joking, laughing, and mocking others. While we were sitting with each other, one of the residents of our neighbourhood came in a beautiful white suit and looked very nice, but he wasn't acting normally. It was Agha Kazem, a truck driver and my neighbour. He was staggering forwards and was on his way home. It was clear he had drunk alcohol and was drunk. When he came closer to us, he suddenly fell into a gutter. We were laughing at him and I was thinking to myself, "It serves him right!" No one went forward [to help him]. In that state, he vomited, and his clothes became dirtier. While we were watching him, Ibrahim came. When he realised what was going on, he went into the gutter and brought Agha Kazem out. Ibrahim got some water and started to clean him. When he became relatively clean, he carried him on his back and started to take him home. I followed Ibrahim. Agha Kazem's house was on Hakimzadeh Street, close to Bab al-Jannah Mosque. Ibrahim knocked on the door and took him inside. Agha Kazem's wife and children were very religious and observed the hijab. Ibrahim put him down on the bench in their courtyard and didn't say anything about what he had done. He then said goodbye and signalled to us to not say anything. In this manner, he saved the reputation of an entire family.

The Grave

My brother was martyred in the operation to liberate Khorramshahr and we buried him in the 26th sector of Behesht-e Zahra. During his funeral, I saw Ibrahim Hadi had come on a motorcycle with one of his friends. Ibrahim's mother was my paternal cousin and Shaheed Mahdi Khandan was my maternal cousin. His leg had been wounded and he was walking on a crutch. When he came closer to the grave, he started to recite eulogies. There was such a beautiful atmosphere. He was reciting with exemplary sincerity and we enjoyed his recitation. As he was leaving, he pointed at my brother's grave and said, "He's been buried in such a great place! I also want my grave to be here, next to Shaheed Hasan Serajiyan Insha'Allah, so whoever passes by on this road will remember us." This sentence stayed in my mind until years later when an unknown martyr was buried in the empty space beside my brother. When Ibrahim's memorial was built next to my brother, I was amazed and asked Ibrahim's family, "Did you choose this place for the memorial?" but they said no. However, I was sure that he had wished for it himself.

Wilayatul Faqih

On the 14th of November 2009, I wanted to go to work earlier than usual, but I was feeling very sleepy. I fell asleep next to the heater for a few moments and suddenly, I was standing in front of the gates of the University of Tehran! A crowd was shouting slogans inside the university. I looked in front of the gate and noticed Ibrahim, Javad Afrasyabi and Reza Goudini standing next to each other and looking at the gate of the university, enraged. I was glad to see my friends after such a long time and I wanted to go to them, but they were so angry, I didn't dare to do so! I woke up. This dream was only a few minutes long, but I couldn't understand what was happening. I called one of my friends who lived close to the university and asked, "What's happening at the gate of the university?" He replied, "Just now, a group of seditious people ripped a large photo of Ayatollah Khamenei and swore at him." I understood the reason for the presence of the martyrs; Ibrahim held the concept of Wilayatul Faqih in extremely high regard.

THE DEFENDERS OF THE SHRINE

Without a doubt, if Ibrahim was present during the sorrowful conditions in the Middle East today, apart from starting cultural activities, he would join the defenders of the Revolution's sanctity. On the Iranian New Year last year, I went for *ziyarah* in Iraq. The day I reached Karbala, I did *ziyarah* on behalf of Ibrahim and prayed for him. That night, I had a dream that a large crowd had gathered in Bayn al-Haramayn like they would in a religious gathering. I went in as well and sat in a corner. I suddenly noticed Ibrahim was sitting across from me, his face luminous as ever. I wanted to go over to him, but I felt shy. I asked the person giving out tea, "Is he Ibrahim Hadi?" He said yes and I asked, "What's he doing in Iraq?" The man replied whispered, "He is (Shaheed) Haj Qassem

Soleimani's[41] consultant." Within those few days, the Iraqi warriors liberated the city of Tikrit which was considered as a stronghold for ISIS with the least amount of losses, all by the intercession of our mother, Lady Zahra (a).

Many of the martyred Defenders of the Shrines loved Ibrahim Hadi. Shaheed Mahdi Azizi always had a photo of Ibrahim in his pocket, he had read his book and whenever he saw a photo of him, he would say salaam to him.

Shaheed Sayyid Mostafa Sadrzadeh made his military codename Sayyid Ibrahim. He would always buy Ibrahim's book, write inside, "Read and pass along," and would give it to others.

Shaheed Sayyid Milad Mostafavi would go to the Kumayl Trench whenever he could and have private time with Ibrahim.

Whenever Shaheed Abbas Daneshgar would see one of his professors who fought alongside Ibrahim, he would ask him to say a few words about him.

Shaheed Hadi Zolfaghari is one who doesn't need an introduction. He had made his military codename Ibrahim Hadi Zolfaghari. Ibrahim had been his Hadi his whole life.

Shaheed Ali Omaraei had read all his books and took a photo of himself with Ibrahim's memorial as a keepsake.

Shaheed Haj Hameed Asadollahi was in love with Ibrahim and concentrated on some of the stories which had a greater moral.

Shaheed Mohammad Kamran was one of the residents of Ibrahim's neighbourhood, had made him his role model and walked in Ibrahim's footsteps.

Shaheed Mahdi Nowruzi had a great love for Ibrahim and I had heard many memories of Ibrahim's life from him.

One of the commanders of the Fatemiyoun Brigade[42] contacted us and said, "We need books for when the soldiers

---

41 Shaheed Lieutenant Qassem Soleimani was an Iranian senior military officer in the IRGC and the commander of its Quds Force. He was martyred in a US drone strike on his military convoy on the 3rd of January 2020.

42 A brigade of Afghani soldiers fighting against the ISIS and Al-Nusra in Iraq and Syria

are bored," so we gave them many books, including *'Peace be upon Ibrahim'* as a gift. Later, we heard a lot about the blessings of Ibrahim's presence amongst the Defenders of the Shrine. On the programme for the Day of Youth, Mortaza Ataei, one of the directors of the Fatemiyoun Brigade, was present. He was one of the veteran Defenders of the Shrine and was praised by Agha Panahian during the programme. Mortaza was also in love with Ibrahim and a while later, he joined the caravan of the martyrs.

www.ingramcontent.com/pod-product-compliance
Lightning Source LLC
Chambersburg PA
CBHW060605080526
44585CB00013B/695